THE DARWIN CONSPIRACY

THE DARWIN CONSPIRACY

A NOVEL BY

JAMES SCOTT BELL

VISION™ HOUSE PUBLISHING, INC.

Gresham, Oregon

THE DARWIN CONSPIRACY

©1995 by James Scott Bell

Published by Vision House Publishing, Inc.
1217 NE Burnside, Suite 403
Gresham, Oregon 97030

Printed in the United States of America

International Standard Book Number: 1-885305-16-8

95 96 97 98 99 00 01 02 03 04 - 10 9 8 7 6 5 4 3 2 1

I am indebted, first and foremost, to John Van Diest, founder of Vision House. He, along with his son, David, caught the "vision" of this project from the start. Doug Halvorson of Vision House was also very encouraging.

The enthusiasm and generosity of my editor, Gloria Kempton, was likewise heartening. She was a joy to work with, and I thank her for her support and inspiration.

Three others who provided significant commentary during various stages of this manuscript were Tom and Beth Hoener and Tom Ellsworth.

And finally, a loving cup of gratitude to my wife, Cindy, who not only made several helpful suggestions, but continued to live with me throughout the writing of this book.

The Busby manuscript fell into my hands through the following remarkable set of circumstances.

I had long entertained the romantic notion that the document, authored by the mysterious figure Sir Max Busby, actually existed, if only because it added a little sparkle and mystery to life. Having studied biology in college with Dr. Hans Hinkel, one of the country's leading evolutionary theorists, I had immersed myself for a time in the lore of evolutionism as well as the so-called "scientific data."

That lore included the possible existence of Sir Max Busby's own account of the history of the theory of evolution.

Of Busby himself very little was known. We could surmise he was an acquaintance of Darwin's. Darwin makes reference to him in a letter to his brother Erasmus (calling him "Dear Max" and "that rascal Busby," the context indicating affection). And we knew he was a historian of sorts. But that was about it.

Some time in the 1920s, a rumor bloomed to the

effect that Busby knew a lot more about the cultural takeover of evolution than was first supposed. And rumor became myth. I discovered that scientists love myth just as much as the rest of us, so long as it accords with their particular world view. Thus, at cocktail parties across the land university science professors, loosed from civilized convention by too much drink, voiced fanciful notions of being the one to find the Busby manuscript. The conversation was no different in tone from, say, pious archaeologists dreaming of Atlantis.

Upon graduation from college I worked a few years and then entered law school, earning my degree in 1984. I joined a law firm and focused my attention on billing clients and getting ahead in the profession.

But always, somewhere in the back of my mind, the possible existence of the Busby manuscript haunted me.

A few years went by, during which time my interest in evolution produced an unexpected turn. I will not bore the reader with the details. Suffice it to say I discovered that the case for Darwinism was virtually nonexistent. I had been hoodwinked by institutions of higher education. Disturbed by this, I tossed my old college textbooks away and stopped thinking about the Busby manuscript altogether.

Then, four years ago, it happened.

An editorial appeared in the *Los Angeles Times*, a paper determined to be wrong in virtually every important subject. This piece was the response to a movement among Christians seeking to mandate balanced treatment in public school classrooms on the matter of origins. The editorial ridiculed this movement, painting all participants as anti-intellectual rubes, and went on to rehash the standard fluff about evolution as established fact.

I responded with a letter, which the *Times* published. I wrote, in part, "It is almost as if a giant conspiracy exists among naturalistic scientists and a willfully blind media to keep the real facts from the public." It is that line, I believe, which prompted the phone call I received the next night.

"Is this James Scott Bell?" a reedy, warbling voice said. I made it out to be a woman, well advanced in years.

"Yes."

"The James Scott Bell who wrote that letter to the *Times?*"

"One and the same. Who is this?"

"You must come see me. Tomorrow...427 River Street."

"Why must I come see you? Who—" *Click.* The line went dead.

I might have dismissed this as a crank call, perhaps from some ardent evolutionist bent on revenge. But something told me this wasn't the case and I decided to follow up.

I arrived at 427 River Street the next morning at ten o'clock. It was an old style house, built in the twenties I supposed, touched up through the years. The neighborhood was quiet, a little dreary. It was a cloudy day.

I knocked on the door. A peephole opened and an eye appeared. The eye had a voice attached to it. "Yes?" It was the same voice I'd heard over the phone.

"I'm James Bell," I said.

The peephole slammed shut. A lock and chain were undone from inside. The door slowly creaked open.

She was old, all right, thin and stooped over, wearing her wrinkled skin like a dress that had once fit but was now too large. The house was dark, the curtains drawn.

For several moments she did not say anything, only looked me over, up and down. Finally she nodded her head slowly and said, "You'll have to do."

Exasperated, I asked her what the meaning of this summons was. I thought a little show of authority would help. She was not impressed. She simply lifted a bony finger to her lips, then used the same finger to indicate that I follow her.

Up the stairs we went. I didn't think she could make the climb. But she never stopped, just took her time. The stairs creaked a haunting melody as we ascended. We made our way to a door at the end of the hall. The old woman reached into the pocket of her dress and produced a key, unlocked the door.

The room smelled musty. Only the dust seemed fresh.

"Listen, madam," I said, "I really want to know—"

Her finger pointed to an antique bureau on top of which sat a framed photograph. I took a closer look. It was a very old man, dressed in twenties garb, in front of what I judged to be this very house. I told her I didn't recognize the gentleman.

She told me his name was Sir Max Busby.

Sir Max Busby? Fabled author of the Busby manuscript? My head went light on me, and I had to sit down. My first thought was that this was some sort of hoax. But I couldn't think of any reason why this woman should lie to me. So I merely whispered in a somber tone, "So that's really Sir Max?"

"Then you know what this is about?" the old woman said.

"The manuscript?"

She nodded, then proceeded to tell me how she had become Max's housekeeper near the end of his life. This house had been his, recorded under a false name. This was necessitated because Max was convinced his life was in danger. He had spent his last year of life working on the manuscript.

At that point, the old woman opened a bureau drawer and pulled out a hand bound sheaf of pages. It had a brown, heavy paper cover, and was flaking around the edges. A shoelace held the pages together by way of two holes punched through the manuscript. She brought it out gingerly, reverently, and handed it to me.

Then she said, "His instructions were that I give this to the right person, one who would believe what is written here, and who also had enough influence in the community to do something about it. By the way, what do you do for a living?"

"I'm a lawyer," I said.

She sighed. "Well, you'll have to do."

"Thank you."

"I am old, and don't have much time left. I must give this manuscript up now, and pray to God that it be used rightly. That's where you come in. This has eternal consequences."

"What are you trying to tell me?" I asked.

She smiled softly, but her eyes were deeply somber, as if the future of the human race were reflected in those ancient orbs. "Don't blow it," she said.

That's how I met Florence Crookshank, Sir Max's nurse at the end of his life, and received the document that would mark an end to my tranquil existence as a mild mannered attorney without an enemy in the world.

That night, with trembling fingers, I opened the yellowed pages of the legendary Busby Manuscript—the first-hand account of the Darwin conspiracy—and began to read...

James Scott Bell

Los Angeles, California

The Busby Manuscript

I

I Sir Max Busby, knighted by the queen, in control of all my faculties save for a few minor physical ones, do hereby set pen to paper, for what will probably be the last time.

This is my confession.

May God have mercy on my soul.

I am 127 years old. I do not know why I have lived so long. I might have said, at one time, "It's in the genes." But I don't say such things anymore, and you will know why, by and by. It would have been better for mankind, I think, if I had not lived 127 years, nor seventeen, nor even seven.

Why not? you may ask. I shall tell you.

At age seven I committed my first act of deliberate cruelty.

At seventeen I murdered my father.

And at 127 one could almost say I murdered the human race.

You can do a lot in 127 years, I'll tell you that.

They are looking for me, of course. That is why I must write as much as I can, before they find me. When they do I know what will happen. One accident will cancel out another. The strongest accident will survive.

That's the way they will put it, anyway. I know better than that now.

I feel that I will only be able to write, at the most, half an hour a day. My strength, what there is left of it, will be gone soon. Thank God for Florence who makes my life so much easier.

Another thing: My mind does not always operate chronologically. Memories inject themselves for no apparent reason.

Like this one: I am standing in front of a painting in the spring of 1913. It appears to be a collection of old cans. But it is supposed to be a nude descending a staircase. How do I know this? Because the title is *Nude Descending a Staircase*. The painter is a fellow named Duchamp. He is what they call a cubist. I am told that for artists like this, "anything goes." There is no need to represent reality. There are no standards that one must be a slave to.

In other words, evolutionary theory has reached even the world of art. And I am supposed to be happy.

Bear with me.

II

I was born Thomas Fairbank in Shropshire, England, February 12, 1809.

I was the last of six children, the only boy. My mother died giving me life.

My father Edgar Fairbank, a successful doctor, was influenced in his perceptions toward me because of my mother's death. My earliest recollection is of him calling me a "despicable worm." I must have been five or six at the time.

He hired a nanny to take care of his children, a shrewish woman named Zenobia Pesterling, who looked like a cross between a ferret and an ox cart. I don't recall her ever smiling, except once during a severe beating I received at the hands of my father when I was eight.

My father married Zenobia when I was nine.

At the marriage ceremony I remember asking myself this question: "Is all of this an accident, or does God want it this way?"

God was talked about in our household. We were required to gather nightly in the study, while my father read to us from a big, black Bible.

He had a few favorite stories.

One of them was about the youths who called the prophet Elisha "thou bald head." God produced a bear to rip them to shreds. At this point in the story, Father always looked directly at me and described the probable medical details of such an attack.

"First," he would say, "your windpipe is ripped open"—he always said "your" as if to place me in the story—"and you suck and gasp for air, but you cannot get any. Blood spurts from your neck. And then the bear claws your abdomen and tears it wide, and he bites you on the shoulders and back and after you are dead, the carrion eating birds pick apart your bones."

Then he would add, "And that's what God will do to you, if you do not obey your father."

Another favorite story of my father's was the slaughter of the prophets of Baal, how they were taken into the Kishon Valley and summarily eliminated.

"And that is what God will do with you, if you do not obey your father."

I soon got the idea that obeying my father was my means of survival. I also got the idea that God was someone I would rather not meet in a dark alley.

Once, at the age of six, I made the mistake of asking Father a question. "Why is God so mean?"

He drew himself up and filled his body with air, his eyes bulging like hen's eggs. "How dare you ask such a thing!"

I was taken into the barn and beaten with a buggy whip.

That was the last time I ever asked my father a question.[1]

But I did continue to ask myself questions, and I did come up with some answers. Was this God a friend to my father? Then I did not care to be a friend to this God. Was this God the author of what the world called "goodness"? Then I did not want any part of that goodness. Was I really a miserable sinner in the eyes of God and my father? Then I would be the best sinner who ever lived.

Little did I realize just how far my sins would take me.

The next morning I packed the manuscript carefully into my briefcase and drove to UCLA. I hadn't bothered to make an appointment with Dr. Hans Hinkle. One would not be necessary once I told him what I had in my possession.

His office door was open. I could hear him conversing in his distinctive German accent. "Natural selection is therefore a principle of local adaptation, not of general advance or progress," he was saying. I recognized the statement as part of his general "punctuated equilibrium" class, the one where he attempted to make coherent a theory that is really nothing more than a scientific three shell game.

A young woman, presumably an undergraduate

who didn't know any better, asked, "But didn't Darwin's theory predict the gradual transition of lower forms into higher forms?"

"Yes," said Hinkle, with what we used to call the "Hinkle twinkle" in his voice.

"Then," said the student, "new species are not created gradually, through mutation?"

"Correct."

"Then how does evolution happen?"

"We don't know."

"But...when I enrolled here, I was under the impression we did know how evolution takes place."

"That is the public perception," said Hinkle, "perpetuated by popular media and pseudo-scientific publicity hounds. Real scientists admit there are many things we still don't know."

I stuck my head in the office door. "And there is no way of knowing just how much we don't know, is there?"

Dr. Hinkle looked up. It took him a second, but he recognized me. "Bell? Is that you?"

"One and the same."

"Come in, my boy, come in!" he said, giving me his full attention.

"I thought science had all the answers," she said weakly as she quietly withdrew from the office.

"Smart girl," Hinkle said. "But I'm afraid her easily held beliefs are shattering."

"How would you like a little shattering of your own?"

Hinkle squinted at me.

He was a short, stocky man of seventy, with bushy eyebrows and thinning white hair that seemed to obey its own peculiar laws of physics. His clothes were rumpled, though he wore a carefully knotted tie.

I closed the door. Hinkle lit up his ever present cigar. "What have you been doing with yourself?"

"A little of this, a little of that. Practicing law, rejecting evolutionary theory, you know—same old."

He nodded through the cloud of cigar smoke. "I see. Like so many others these days. You do have a scientifically viable alternative to propose, don't you?"

"Yes. Intelligent design."

"Bah!" said Hinkle, waving the brown stogie in the air. "Metaphysical nonsense. I would have thought better of a former student of mine."

"Still claiming all science must be based on

naturalism, eh professor?"

"Of course! It must be! Without naturalism, all of science would crumble. We would have no parameters."

"So we continue to insist that blind, natural causation is all there is in the world, when the reality may be that the supernatural does, in fact, exist."

An impatient puff of smoke issued from the professor. "I'm not a philosopher, only a scientist. I must have proof that I can see."

I smiled, and allowed myself a "twinkle" of my own. "What if I told you I had proof that the entire evolutionary theory was 'metaphysical nonsense' from the start?"

"Proof?"

"Yes."

His stare was inquisitorial. "I'd say, 'Prove it.' "

I gingerly placed my briefcase on my lap. "Dr. Hinkle, when I was a student of yours I remember you talking about Sir Max Busby. You were one of the leading experts on him, I believe."

"I still am, my boy. He is a passion of mine."

"And I remember you telling us about the Busby manuscript."

A sad, longing look brushed over his face. "The stuff of legend."

"Legend?"

"I'm convinced now it doesn't really exist. If it did, it would have turned up. Ah, well. It's romantic to think about, no?"

I slowly opened the briefcase case and pulled out the bound pages, holding them as I would a sacred scroll. "Behold the Busby manuscript," I said.

For once Dr. Hans Hinkle, the voluble scholar, was at a loss for words. He stared for a full minute at the document in the open briefcase. Finally he said, "You expect me to believe that?"

"Not yet," I said. "Even I'm having trouble believing it. That's why I'm here. Of all the people in the world who could authenticate this manuscript, you are the one I trust. You are an honest man of science. And you've studied Busby. Before I do anything with it, I have to be sure."

He stood, and came around his desk, approaching slowly. He carefully put down his cigar and held out his hands. "May I?"

I placed the manuscript in his hands and he took it gingerly, hefting it—no doubt pondering it like Aladdin grasping the magic lamp. He turned to the first page and began to read.

As he did, I watched his eyes. They grew progressively wider. Hinkle even began to tremble slightly. Without looking up from the pages he went back to his chair and sat, transfixed.

A few minutes later he looked at me. "It has the sound of Sir Max," he said, in a reverent whisper. "And the paper is old, like my father's original copy of *Elbert Hubbard's Scrapbook.*" He went to his bookshelf and pulled down a brown paper, string-bound book with the same dimensions as the Busby manuscript. *Elbert Hubbard's Scrapbook* was a popular collection of quotations, published in 1923. It had the same look and feel as the manuscript Hinkle now held in his hands.

"Then you think this might be the real thing?" I said.

"The theory," Hinkle said slowly, "is plausible. Tell me, would you allow me to read it tonight, more closely?"

"I don't know..."

"Please."

"To be honest, I don't want to let this out of my sight. It was given to me in confidence."

Hinkle frowned. "Let me keep it for today then," he said. "I will lock my door behind you and the manuscript will not leave my office. You can come back for it at exactly six o'clock."

I hesitated.

"I give you my word of honor that I will not leave this office until you have returned," he said.

Hans Hinkle was a scientist with a reputation for the highest integrity. Wherever the truth led, that is the path he followed. And it was of the utmost importance to authenticate the Busby manuscript. I would not be able to do anything with it unless I had independent corroboration.

But something in Hinkle's disposition gave me pause. He seemed nervous all of a sudden, unlike the deliberate, confident instructor I'd always known him to be. I wondered for a moment if there was something more in all this, something Hinkle understood but was not willing to reveal. Then again, perhaps it was an overactive imagination on my part. Naturally Hinkle would be a bit unstrung. He'd just received what was, for him, the equivalent of the Holy Grail.

I left the manuscript with him and drove back to my office. Traffic was light on the Ventura Freeway, an occurrence as rare as transitions in the fossil record. I passed a car sporting a Christian fish symbol that had little legs and "Darwin" written across it. I chuckled at this, as I always do. What better evidence of the fact that Darwinism is itself a faith, as zealously guarded as any form of fundamentalism?

I hadn't been at my office ten minutes before my secretary buzzed the intercom.

"A Mr. Joel Nairobi to see you."

Nairobi? I wasn't expecting anyone by that name. But a potential client is a potential client. "Show him in," I said.

Nairobi was a small boned man of medium height. His hair was black and smooth and very glossy. He was dressed in a snugly tailored suit, and wore, of all things, gloves. His features were exotic, Moroccan I guessed. He smelled of gardenia.

"Please have a seat, Mr. Nairobi."

Nairobi bowed elegantly and said "I thank you," in a high pitched voice. He sat down primly, crossing his ankles, and began to draw off his gloves.

"Now what can I do for you, Mr. Nairobi?"

"It is my understanding, Mr. Bell, that you may be in possession of a certain, shall we say, item. An item which holds a great deal of significance for a certain, shall we say, party?"

I sat back in my chair, trying not to look stunned. "And what sort of item would that be?"

"A document—a manuscript if you will—of very old vintage."

I felt perspiration erupt on my palms, and blood rush to my cheeks. I tried to keep my twitching jaw from giving away the store.

"I don't think I follow you, Mr. Nairobi. Please explain more about this...speculation."

Nairobi smiled and looked coyly at the floor. "Mr. Bell, the party I represent does not speculate. It is not in her interest."

"Her?"

"That is all I am prepared to say, except that I am authorized to pay you the sum of fifty thousand dollars for the manuscript. And I am prepared to promise that—what is the phrase?—no questions will be asked."

"Fifty thousand dollars is a lot of money. It—"

A buzz came over the phone. "Yes?" I said.

"I'm going to lunch now," Effie said.

"See you in an hour."

I turned to face Nairobi again. "Like I was saying, that's a lot of money."

Nairobi smiled, then took a short, compact black pistol out of an inner pocket. "You will please," he said, "clasp your hands at the back of your neck."

III

When I was seven years old, I committed my first act of premeditated evil. I remember the act vividly, and equally vividly do I remember the joy I felt at its accomplishment.

There was a girl in our town named Mary Stuart, the daughter of the schoolteacher. She was my age.

Everyone spoke of her as if she were God's gift to the village. That alone was enough to make me loathe her. She had golden hair, blue eyes, and a smile like a spring morning. She pranced through life as if it were some sort of glorious dream.

I decided to wake her up.

Mary followed the same path to and from school every day. It was a path that took her around the outskirts of our town, by the dairy fences, along a quaint little road dotted with wildflowers.

One day after school, I ran ahead of the other children and took a place on top of a hill, overlooking the road.

The hill held deposits of fine Shropshire ironstone. I found a piece the size of a goose egg, and upon examination, was delighted to find that it had a sharp point jutting from one side. I positioned myself behind a bush and waited.

It did not take long for Mary to come skipping down

the road. She held a basket, pausing every now and then to pick a flower and place it inside. She seemed full of wonder at what she supposed to be God's creation.

My aim was perfect. The rock sailed through the misty air, twirling with malicious accuracy. The thud when it met Mary's head was exquisite to me—like a hammer hitting a melon, or a brick dropped upon a butter churn. The point must surely have found its place, for a gush of red immediately visited itself on the golden slopes of her head. Following closely thereafter was a wail of such haunting despair, such horrible agony, such sudden desolation, that my soul felt full and complete.

I watched her fall, wailing, to the ground, and then I ran.

They never found out who did it. And Mary Stuart was never the same after that. It was as if a demon had reached inside her and ripped from her body whatever hope of happiness in childhood she might have had.

I was that demon.

IV

Life at home grew intolerable. My father beat me regularly.

I responded by withdrawing more and more into myself, where I could inhabit a world ruled by force and terror. Every now and again I would supplement it with reality and do something evil to give myself a boost.

Such as setting fire to Jonathan Millard's barn. Several horses and two cows died.

Or robbing silver candlesticks from the church rectory.

Sometimes, I thought of committing murder but held back. I wanted to wait until I could fully savor it, appreciate it completely, plan it out perfectly. But just the contemplation of it made me joyful. I had found my true calling, if you will; my true source of happiness: evil.

I slid into my teenage years with all the serpentine confidence of a paragon of evil. The course of my life was set, and how many young men at my age could say as much? I looked forward to an adulthood of bad deeds.

And then one day an odd and terrible thing occurred which threatened to upset my happily demented spirit.

It was in my seventeenth year, and I was walking down a country road just after poisoning a herd of pigs. The day was sunny, and I was whistling a merry little tune. Suddenly I heard another sound, one that should have sent me into greater heights of well-being, a noise I would have been proud at any time to have instigated, namely, a scream.

Yes, someone was screaming around the bend. From what I could determine it was the shriek of a young boy.

Hurrying my step, I came into view of the scene. Three young hooligans had set upon a lad, who looked to be about ten years old, and were tormenting him, throwing dirt at him, slapping him, laughing and spitting at him in a merriment of abuse. They did not appear to be desirous of anything but making the little boy as miserable as possible.

My first instinct was to sit and enjoy the spectacle. But the trio of thugs looked up from their project, saw me, and took off running. No doubt they suspected I was a virtuous adult determined to bring them to justice. I almost called them back but let it go. I kept walking toward the petrified child, now clinging to his knees on the ground.

Maybe I'd enjoy a little kick or two myself before I went on my way. Perhaps I would simply abuse the boy verbally, tell him how evil the world really was and assure him this life held no hope of happiness. I wasn't sure what I would do, I only knew it would be something wonderfully aberrant.

And then, as I was just about to commence, I stopped cold. For I found, with considerable shock, that I was looking down at myself.

The boy had rolled over when he heard my footsteps. His face was dirty, wet from tears and spittle and sweat.

But there was no mistaking the resemblance between the youth and the once boyish Thomas Fairbank.

It was not so much in the features, though they were similar indeed. It was in the eyes—fearful, distant, as if gazing into a blackness of impenetrable depth.

"Please, sir!" he cried out. "Please don't hit me! I'll get a whippin' sure already!"

"What are you jabbering about?" I said, as rudely as I could manage.

"My papa, sir. He'll give me a taste of the Inferno, he will, for messing up me clothes." He wiped his nose with a forearm, and trembled.

"Your father whips you?"

"'Course he does. He's me father, after all."

"So?"

"He has the right, he does. And me, bein' the miserable bugger that I am, jus' another mouth to feed, he has good cause, too."

I cannot explain all that happened within me at that moment, but it was something that frightened me to the depths of my rotten core. It was something that I can only describe as...compassion.

Compassion! Can you imagine a more untoward feeling a committed evildoer can experience? And yet, there it was, and before I could reason out all of the implications, I was helping the unfortunate child to his feet and brushing the dust off his clothes.

I even put my arm around his shoulder to help him walk the first few steps toward the nearest town. His name was Willie.

We proceeded to the place of business of the town doctor where I placed Willie for observation. Almost of its own accord, my right hand went into my trousers and pulled out a few coins which I put in the doctor's hand. "Take care of the boy," I said and slipped out the door as fast as I could.

It was nightfall by the time I reached my village. By then I was fully in agony at the events which had just transpired.

What was it? Some force within me attempting to draw me away from evil toward the thing I hated most, goodness? Where would such a force come from?

God? Terrible prospect! A perverse trick played by my enemy. Imagine, planting within me a desire toward charity. There could be no greater torment for a confirmed blasphemer!

The worst was yet to come.

For several weeks after this encounter, I was unable to sleep. I had dreams—nightmares—in which I offered a host of good deeds to unfortunate sufferers. Torture it was indeed!

And then Willie found me. He showed up on my doorstep one day, rapping on the door.

"At last I found you," he said, smiling.

"What do you want?" I answered brusquely.

"I want you to have something for your kindness."

Raising my face to the sky, I let out a wail of profound anguish.

"Are you all right, sir?" the boy asked. "Need a doctor?"

"No!" I snapped. I wanted to slam the door in the boy's face but found I could not.

He reached into his jacket, pulled out a small object and handed it to me. "Please take it, sir," he said. "It ain't much, but I did it meself."

I snatched the object out of his hand. It was the figure of an angel, sculpted out of the unmistakable blackness of Shropshire ironstone. It had its crude corners and ambiguous details, but there was no mistaking its rough beauty.

A wretched warmth rushed through me and before I could think further, for the first time in my life, I said, "Thank you."

"It'll protect you, I wager," Willie said. "Always." Then he smiled, waved, and ran away. I never saw him again.

Still holding the angel figure, I walked, like a man in a trance, to a desolate hill outside the village. The gray of an ensuing storm began to close in around me. I sat down and began to weep uncontrollably.

My world was turning on end! Was this a call I could no longer ignore? But I had already found my calling.

Hadn't I? It was as if I stood at the fork on an eternal road. Why was this happening to me now? Why?

Determined to find an answer, I pounded on the door of the vicarage until the vicar—a stout old fellow, gray of head and beefy of face—answered.

He must have sensed my desperation, for he immediately put down his flagon of ale and showed me into his study.

"What does God want of me?" I asked.

The vicar thought a moment. "For you to do His will," he said.

"But what is that?"

"To stay free of sin, and to do good works."

"Tell me more about sin."

"The works of the flesh are clearly revealed. Adultery, fornication, uncleanness—"

"So far so good."

"—lustfulness, idolatry, sorcery—"

"Right as rain."

"—hatreds, fightings, jealousies, angers—"

"Hold it." I put my hand up. "Does 'hatreds' mean actually hating someone, a person?"

"Yes."

"And what if one, speaking hypothetically of course, persists in this hate?"

"Those practicing such things will not inherit the kingdom of God."

Of course, I hadn't cared about the kingdom of God up to this point. I imagined it to be little more than bodies of torn flesh wandering around awaiting more torment for disobedience.

Now, suddenly and without warning, I had the incredible thought that perhaps the kingdom of God was something to be desired, and that I should do something about inheriting it.

As I pondered these things, the vicar said, "Thomas, who is it you hate?"

I didn't say anything.

"Your father?" the vicar asked.

I nodded, and looked at my shoes.

"Then you must go to him. You must seek his forgiveness. And then you must seek God's. Do you understand?"

I did not, but I nodded, and left as quickly as I could. The rain had come, and I walked home in it, not caring if I should be washed away to the Severn River and thereupon meet my death. But I knew it would not happen. I knew that presently I would walk in the door and face once again the man I dreaded more than any other human being.

I would make a stab at it. I would ask him to forgive me. For I knew without thinking long on it that it was what I ought to do. A moral imperative had clamped itself upon my heart, for perhaps the first time in my entire, meaningless life.

How would my father react?

I didn't care to guess.

I only knew that, whatever the reaction, it would change my life forever.

V

Father was in his laboratory, fiddling with a femur. He had an impressive collection of human bones, which he often studied.

I apparently disturbed him, for he seemed even more gruff than usual. "What do you want?" he growled.

"Father?" My voice was tentative, weak.

"I said, what do you want?"

"I want to say something."

"Well then, say it." He turned and looked at me. His eyes were like lumps of coal set on fire. This did not surprise me. He often had that look, as if some inner flame of torment were suddenly raised in response to a bellows blast. Most of the time, that look was directed at me.

I shuffled my feet, my own insides burning like a smelting furnace. Hot tears raged into my eyes, and the scene went fuzzy. "Papa," I said, using a name I hadn't employed since I was five years old, "I want you to forgive me."

The words stunned him. He did not move. The fire in his eyes glowed hot and red, but the head remained still. Thinking back on it, I can only surmise that this was such an unexpected utterance from his despised son that it momentarily threw him into a state of disequilibrium. The syntax of forgiveness was unknown to him. Having it come from the target of his unending derision, the source of his hate, simply threw him for a loss.

Still holding the chalk-colored thigh bone, he turned his entire body toward me and said, "What have you done now?"

"Nothing, Papa! I just wanted to say—"

"Come on, out with it! What are you hiding?" His knuckles whitened around the femur.

"Honest, Papa, I haven't done a thing," I squeaked, my voice faltering. "At least, not today."

"Well then when have you?"

I gulped. I remember the feeling of that gulp. It was a swallow of abject torment, of palpable fear, as when a boy is faced with the dread and dark unknown from a person who is his closest human relation, his own flesh and blood. "Papa, I want...want you to forgive me for...harboring bad thoughts about you!"

It was out. The smelting furnace inside me blasted furiously, turning my entire body into a repository of burning organs. I thought for a moment that I would faint, either from heat or fear. But I did not faint.

How I wish now I had.

Father took a single, ominous step toward me. His face showed no understanding, no softening, no mercy.

"I want you to forgive me, Papa," I explained, "and then I want God to forgive me. Please Papa, I want God to forgive me!"

Father froze, and for a moment no sound was heard save for my panting. My destiny hanging in the balance, I quivered. I knew what my father did next would cast my lot for the ages.

What was I expecting? The milk of human kindness? From my father? Yes, in my adolescent mind, that is what I wanted most of all. But it was a pipe dream considering my circumstances.

My father took a step toward me, the femur still clutched in his hand.

A clubbing on the side of my head? That was a more realistic possibility, though I doubted that my father, in view of his standing in the community, would risk the unfortunate demise of his son at his own hands.

But my doubts wavered when he took another menacing step. He gripped the femur harder, as if trying to crush it with his bare hand.

I took a step back, stumbling on discarded bridle, but staying upright.

My father took another step forward.

I backed up to my left, a poor choice, for the door lay in the opposite direction. Behind me now was a bare wall, with an attached work bench jutting out from it.

I was cornered.

My father stepped in front of me so there was no possibility of my scampering out. I trembled like a small laboratory rat, crouching in his imprisoning nook, powerless to stop the giant, approaching hand of the vivisectionist.

My father raised the femur above his head.

I squeezed my eyes shut, put my hands on top of my head and screamed, "No, Papa, no!"

And then it happened.

The unexpected.

I was not coshed upon my head.

I opened one eye.

My father threw the femur on a slab. And then he laughed.

Oh, it was a chilling laugh, a cold and cruel laugh! What one would expect from a crazy house gargoyle in a nightmare from which one struggled to awake—that is the laugh my father laughed.

If there had been any warmth, any decency, any goodness left in my tired, seventeen-year-old soul, that laugh was the poison that killed any possibility of bloom. I could feel the shriveling of my moribund humanity into ugly, repulsive off scouring.

My father's eyes no longer flamed. They didn't need to. Instead they became as black as a Welsh mine. "You little curse," he said. "God shall never forgive you. And neither shall I!"

Do prophets look back in remembrance of the time they heard the call of their God? And do they sometimes, in weak moments, after a hard day's jeremiad, rue the day so heavy a burden was laid upon them? For prophecy is a load to carry, and lamentation an inevitable consequence. But there is always that moment, that great and terrible moment, when the die is cast, when destiny is sealed.

Such a time came for me at the moment my father spoke those words. Two things happened simultaneously in my brain. The first was a conflagration, an eruption of flame, the smelting furnace exploding up into my head, blazing rage consuming the last of any rational faculties emitting faint screams, devouring them like the lava of a volcano gormandizing sacrificial virgins.

The second thing was a peace which told me all was well. With no uncertainty at all, I knew that the God of my father would be my eternal enemy, giving me a purpose for living. The battle was joined. I would be the new Lucifer.

I grabbed the femur from the slab with two fists and swung it with all my might.

A sea of red erupted from my father's skull. He crumpled to the ground, like a puppet whose strings are suddenly snipped.

I figured him to be dead, but just to make sure I gave him twenty more good ones.

Outside, the rain had subsided, and golden rays of sunlight began to stream through the windows.

VI

I had to make myself scarce. Thus began five years of wandering—becoming a fugitive and vagabond in the earth.

I changed my name to Max Busby. This had to do with a traveling dog act I'd seen once, in which a trainer named Max had a dog named Busby dance around on his hind legs. He accomplished this with the deft snap of a whip. The symbolism was not lost on me, so I took on the new name.

Eventually, I worked my way to Plymouth, surviving through cunning and theft. I committed a few murders here and there but nothing to speak of.

Then three incidents occurred that changed the course of my life.

The first was finding my photo posted on the wall of the Plymouth constabulary. "Wanted for the murder of Edgar Fairbank," my father. And not a bad likeness of me, put together as it must have been by an artist working with the recollections of my Shropshire neighbors.

So the information had spread this far. My case was still "open."

The second incident was finding that same poster in some of the local pubs. The price I was fetching would buy quite a number of rounds.

The third incident was having my head clunked from behind by a table leg in the hands of an old gaffer who was interested in those rounds. Luckily I survived, and it being foggy and dark, and the chap sufficiently in his cups, I was able to slip away. But it appeared I had to leave England.

I remembered something I'd heard in a pub a few nights before. Two old salts, with a palpable fish stench that practically spoiled my ale, were talking about signing on a ship bound for Teirra del Fuego and then coming home by the East Indies—a veritable around-the-world cruise.

I had thought that information might come in handy some day. Now it did.

I inquired at the docks and was directed to the ship where I requested a spot. I needed qualifications, of course, but that was easy. I lied.

And so, in December 1831, I was signed on as a cook aboard a ten-gun, 235-ton sloop-brig under the command of Captain Robert FitzRoy, RN.

The name of the ship was *HMS Beagle*.

Unbeknownst to me at the time, the ship had taken on what they called a "naturalist," someone the captain wanted to help him examine the metal rich Fuegian mountains.

Later, I learned the name of this chap from another sailor. I thought he said this naturalist was a "Charles Durbin."

VII

It was Charles Darwin, of course, the man, the seer, the sower, the key.

Darwin, mover of mountains, spinner of webs, chaser of bugs.

Darwin, loved, hated, revered, reviled.

Darwin, filer of nature and changer of history.

This was the Darwin who would become the lever I needed, like Archimedes, to move the world.

No one knows the real story.

Now they will.

"Where is the manuscript?" Nairobi said, pointing the little pistol at my head. "I warn you that if you do not tell me where it is I will certainly shoot you."

My head swirled. "What...what is this all about?"

"The manuscript!"

"I don't have anything here you'd be interested in."

Sighing, Nairobi said, "You will please stand and

move to the center of the room. I have to make sure you are not armed."

"Armed?"

"I intend to search your office. Now if you please."

Knees wobbly, I did as I was told. Nairobi puttered behind me and started to pat me down. The scene was beginning to take on aspects of the absurd. Why was he after the manuscript? How did he find out I had it?

What would stop him from shooting me anyway? The scene may have been absurd, but it was also potentially deadly. I glimpsed, in my mind's eye, a picture of me laying in a pool of blood.

Fear has a funny effect on people. On me, it resulted in a quick spin, my elbow angled outward. I caught Nairobi across the face. He collapsed to the floor, unconscious.

Breathing hard, my temples pounding, I grabbed the revolver and breathed a silent prayer of gratitude. I started ruffling through Nairobi's pockets, working methodically. There was a wallet, an airplane ticket receipt showing San Francisco to L.A., and a box of Altoid mints. I called the police.

Nairobi awakened slowly. Finally, he focused on me sitting on the edge of my desk, pointing the revolver at him. Then he looked down and spotted blood. "Look what you've done to my shirt!"

"Sorry, but what am I supposed to do when you come in with a phony offer, then threaten me with a gun?"

Clearing his throat, Nairobi said, "I assure you my offer was genuine."

"Who is the offer from?"

"Forgive me for not answering that question, Mr. Bell."

Frustrated, I shouted, "I just want to know what's going on! Look, I'm new at this game, but if you don't give me some answers this thing may go off."

Nairobi straightened his shirt and began putting on his gloves. "Let me put it this way, Mr. Bell. You are in over your head. You may have temporarily disarmed me, but this is not the end, shall we say, of the story. May I have my gun back please?"

"Sorry. The police wouldn't like that."

"Police! You called the police?"

"Brandishing a weapon at a citizen is a no-no in this state."

Nairobi's eyes bulged. "You...you!"

"I can recommend a decent attorney, though."

Nairobi didn't find this at all comforting. I was forced to hold him at gun point until the police arrived. He refused to talk to me or answer any of my questions. But I did have time to think.

My first concern was Dr. Hinkle. If this character Nairobi knew about the manuscript, and was willing to kill for it, it was likely someone in league with him might be paying a visit to Hinkle, too. Maybe that was why Hinkle had seemed so nervous. Keeping an eye on Nairobi, I dialed Hinkle's office. He didn't answer the phone.

After asking me countless questions, the police took Nairobi away. I hopped into my Taurus and zipped back to the campus. I parked and raced to the science building. I was stopped short at the hallway leading to Hinkle's office. There was yellow police tape everywhere.

A sergeant was standing guard. "What happened?" I asked, trying to control the shaking in my voice.

"There's been a murder," he answered. "College professor."

"Murder? Who was it?"

"I can't give you any info."

"Was it Dr. Hans Hinkle?"

Squinting, the sergeant said, "What do you know about it?"

"I was one of the last to see him alive. Better take me to the man in charge."

The sergeant walked me down the hall toward Hinkle's office. There were signs of a struggle. Photographers were taking pictures and medical examiners and detectives were sorting through the mess. I could feel the color draining from my face. The sergeant called over a Lieutenant Dundy, a tough-looking bird, dropped me in front of him, and explained my presence.

"You saw him this morning?" Dundy said.

"Yes."

"Why?"

"I used to be a student of his."

"Just a friendly chat?"

"I wanted his opinion on something."

"What was that?"

"I wanted him to look at a manuscript."

"Uh-huh," Dundy said, unwrapping a stick of Juicy Fruit. "You have any idea why he was murdered?"

"How do you know it was murder?" I asked.

"He came stumbling out of his office with a knife in his back, calling for help, then collapsed right over there."

"I was in his office just a few hours ago. Maybe if I have a look I can give you a lead."

Reluctantly, Dundy let me into Hinkle's office. I was desperate to find the manuscript, but expected the worst. I'd left my briefcase with Hinkle, and it was still on his desk, open but empty. My heart hit my feet like a bad fighter hits the canvas.

"So?" Dundy said.

"It appears that..." I stopped short, and almost lost my breath. There, in the corner behind Hinkle's desk, jutting out from the leaves of an overturned ficus, was a brown manuscript. "There!" I said.

Dundy responded, and with gloved hands retrieved the book. It was indeed the Busby manuscript. I quickly scanned the bookshelves and floor, and noted what was conspicuously absent.

Somewhere, some murderer and thief was in possession of a vintage copy of *Elbert Hubbard's Scrapbook.* I was pretty sure whoever he was working for was not going to be happy with that little item. Dr. Hans Hinkle had carried off the swindle of a lifetime. I smiled.

But the smile faded when Dundy wouldn't give

me the manuscript. "It goes into evidence," he said.

"But it's mine! I brought it here."

"Sorry. We have rules. You'll get it back when we're good and ready to give it back."

Once again, the Busby manuscript was out of my hands. "Just be careful with it," I pleaded.

"I'm gonna want a full statement from you," said Dundy. "But one thing I wanna know right now. Just before Hinkle died, a janitor overheard his last words."

"What were they?"

"He said, 'The opera is over.' Now what do you think he meant by that?"

"I don't know. Haven't got a clue."

Dundy said, "Well, you'll have plenty of time to think about it, 'cause you're going downtown with me. I have a feeling you have a lot more to tell us."

I didn't like the tone in his voice. "What, precisely, do you mean? You're not considering me a suspect, are you?"

"You have the right," Dundy said, "to remain silent."

VIII

A memory flashes:

It is mid-1920, and I am in America on a lecture tour. As is my wont, I get off the train to see the town and get a feeling about these "rubes" as they are sometimes known. I am in the midwest, just outside of Chicago.

In a watering hole I encounter a handsome young man, stoop shouldered over his bootleg beer. His face holds such promise, and yet such despair. I think he may be ripe for the picking.

I seat myself next to him and strike up a conversation. It develops that this young man is recently home from the Great War where he was an ambulance driver on the Italian front. Now he is wondering what to do with his life. He might like to be a writer, but his parents do not approve. He mumbles a curse word and starts fingering a piece of paper.

"May I?" I inquire, feeling that something very important is written here. He resists, but I offer to buy him another beer, and he slides the paper over to me.

It is a letter, a remarkable bit of bile to my way of thinking. It is from the young man's mother, and it tells him his idling ways are beginning to weigh heavily on his parents. In part, it says, "Unless you, my son, come to yourself, cease your lazy loafing and pleasure seeking, stop trading on your handsome face and neglecting your duties to God and your Savior, Jesus Christ, there is nothing before you..."

I almost gag. The mere mention of the deity and His Son is hateful to me.

"This is a very sick woman," I say, adding quickly, "I'm sorry if I offend."

The young man merely grunts.

"She wants to destroy your youth and vigor, it is quite obvious. All this talk about 'duties to God.' Bosh! Be a writer, my boy, and write about life as it really is! We owe no duties to anyone but ourselves!"

For the first time, the young man looks into my eyes. There is a spark there. "Who are you?"

"A friend," I say. "One who knows. Parents are a plague. They are destroyers. Remember that."

"What's your name?"

"Max Busby." I extend my hand. He takes it.

"Mine's Hemingway," he says. "Ernest Hemingway."

This Hemingway, I believe, has made a mark on the literary scene.[2]

IX

Charles Darwin was a fresh-faced youth, unlike myself; I of rough features etched by years of abuse, evil thoughts, and running from the law.

Our first meeting was at the bow of the *Beagle* one sunset shortly after setting out. Being a galley mate, I was preparing to throw some slop over the side, when I stopped to gaze at the young man silhouetted against the orange horizon. He appeared to be seeking something over the side of the ship.

"What are you looking for, mate?" I said.

He didn't answer. Not in language, at least. A dreadful sound erupted from his form, and I suddenly understood what he was doing folded over the rail.

"A bit of the sea sickness, eh?" I said. "It wasn't my salt pork, was it?"

There followed another bellow of agony. I smiled.

Finally, unsteadily, having accomplished his mission, Darwin stood. His face was the color of palm leaves, but he managed a smile anyway. "That's a little better," he said.

I stared, sizing him up. He shifted his feet. Then, as if to make some idle conversation, he swept at the sunset with his hand. "Isn't God's handiwork a magnificent thing?"

I repressed the urge to throw the bucket of slop at him.

"What makes you think it is the product of God's hand?" I said.

He gave a good-natured laugh, as if I were joking. But when he saw the look on my face, it set him straight. "What can you mean?" he asked.

"I mean what I say. What makes you think it?"

"Why, the Bible says it."

"Does it? And who wrote the Bible?"

"You mean Genesis, wherein we are given the creation account? Moses wrote it, of course. Are you an intellectual?"

I spit. "An atheist."

He seemed the slightest bit impressed, and that changed my opinion of him upward, though only marginally. "An atheist! I've never met so anxious a one before."

"And what are you, if I may ask?"

"A naturalist. I take it upon myself to discover what I can of God's creation." He quickly added, "No offense intended."

There was something different about this one, even with his talk of God. I sensed behind his eyes an indefatigable curiosity, a willingness to go to extreme lengths to examine things that fascinated him. I wondered if I could fascinate him with the idea of atheism. Perhaps I could hook a fish.

I allowed him to speak about himself and encouraged him to talk about his work. He rambled on about this and that. But then he said two things, two very curious things that made my head begin to swim with funny thoughts.

First he spoke of his grandfather, Erasmus Darwin, who had been a speculative thinker, biologist, doctor, and poet. He had authored a two-volume treatise entitled *Zoonomia* which was widely disseminated. It was a book intended to unravel the theory of diseases, but was most remembered, young Charles said, for its view on "perpetual transformations."

"Perpetual *what?*" I asked.

"It's a hypothesis about the evolution of living things."

"Evolution of living things?"

"Yes, you know, change."

"How so?"

"Well it's obvious," said Darwin, "that animals of the same speciation are not uniform. You see differences. How did these changes happen? That is what evolutionary speculation seeks to answer."

A thought struck me, and I tossed it out. "I have often thought that certain persons, usually associated with the diaconate of a local church, appear to have descended from the apes."

I'd intended to get a laugh. But Darwin did not laugh.

I wouldn't learn the significance of this omission until much later.

Instead, he said, "I do not hold with Lamarck, if that's what you're thinking."

"Who's Lamarck?"

Lamarck, Darwin explained, had expounded a theory of speciation based upon inherited traits. A short necked herbivore, for example, stretching to get at some high leaves, made his neck just so much longer. His offspring, therefore, would have longer necks. They would stretch over their lifetimes, have offspring and so on. Eventually, you had a new species, called a giraffe. In other words, a new life form had evolved from some "lower" form which preceded it. Or so the speculation went.

Thus, I was stunned to learn that when I spoke of an ape ancestry for man I had actually uttered a scientific hypothesis given credibility in some quarters!

"Of course," Darwin continued, "no one believes that piffle. Variations are small, and stay within a species. It's interesting to think about, though."

Interesting indeed, thought I.

The second significant thing Darwin spoke of had to do with his naturalistic zeal. It seems he had a thing for beetles. Loved the little buggers. One day as a younger man he was tearing off some bark in a wood, and saw two rare beetles attempting to make an escape. He grabbed one in each hand. Then he spotted a third, a kind he had never seen and therefore could not bear to lose. So he popped the one in his right hand into his mouth.

"Alas," Darwin said, recounting the story to me, "it ejected some intensely acrid fluid, which burnt my tongue so much I was forced to spit it out, and lost it, as well as the third one."

I paused silently for a moment, thinking, "This fellow is passing strange." But I had to admire his extremism. Being a rather extreme person myself—I was, after all, a happy murderer—I was drawn to that same trait in another. Perhaps he could become, in due course, a partner in crime. What crime I did not know, but here was clay to work with.

Darwin excused himself and left me. I threw my slop overboard and returned to my quarters.

That night I dreamed of mobs of people throwing their Bibles into a big bonfire. They were throwing them into the fire and dancing and singing, "We are free! We are free!" The dancing got wilder and wilder, the scene ending in a complete debauch, and the people slowly taking on the form of apes.

I sat up in my bunk, sweating. Thoughts swirled.

What if we did have an ape ancestry? What if it were really true? What would that do to Genesis?

Why, it would wipe it out, completely. For the Bible tells us we were made by God, according to our kinds. The Bible would be shown to be a lie!

And if the Bible was a lie, God was a liar. But if God was a liar, He wouldn't be God! There would be no God! Nature would be the only god!

But then again, what if it were not true? What if there really was a God, and He really did exist, really did create all this?

Then an incredible thought struck me. It made me pant, as if I'd run a mile. This was the thought: It doesn't matter! It does not matter if it's true or not, this evolution from lower forms of life. If enough people *believed* it to be true, they would turn their backs on God! They would throw their Bibles, even if figuratively, into the fire!

Sweat ran down my cheeks and arms. I was having a religious experience, worshipping as I did my own intellect. I was envisioning a plan to murder God Himself!

And this young Darwin, he could be the key.

What if this naturalist came to believe such a shocking theory? Man evolving? What if he formulated some credible sounding scientific hypothesis, based on his observations from this voyage?

Oh, if only it might happen!

If only I could find some way to *make* it happen!

This was the way I was thinking as we reached the arid climes of South America.[3]

X

Captain FitzRoy set to surveying the eastern coasts.

Darwin was allowed to go ashore for weeks at a time, and we'd pick him up hundreds of miles away.

What was he doing? Chasing beetles. And birds and lizards and anything else that caught his eye. Also, he lugged a lot of rocks. This was called geology.

He packaged all this trivia up and sent it back to England.

He made copious notes, apparently taking his work very seriously.

Others were given to making sport of him, in a good-natured way.

I never made sport of him.

Rather, whenever the opportunity presented itself, I attempted to plant in his head the credibility of a purely natural explanation for man's existence, and for the existence of everything.

One day, for instance, I happened upon Darwin with his unimpressive nose in a book. "What do you have there?" I asked.

He showed me the title: *Principles of Geology* by someone named Charles Lyell.

"What significance is this?" I asked.

Darwin seemed eager to talk about it. "Lyell believes the earth to be much older than four thousand years."

"Good for him," I snorted. I too rejected, for obvious reasons, Bishop Ussher's claim that the earth was created at 9:00 A.M., October 23, 4004 B.C.

"He argues that the changes in the earth's surface have taken place gradually, over a great expanse of time."

The implications of this kind of thinking began to dawn on me. "Yes, yes?" I said, egging on the youthful naturalist.

"Which, if it were true, would do away with the necessity of divinely directed catastrophes." He said it calmly, as if it were just a curious bit of trivia.

"Then that's it, isn't it?" I said.

"That's what?"

"The final nail in God's coffin!"

He laughed. "Really, Max, you are such a swine sometimes."

I was undaunted. "Don't you see it, Charles? The evidence is unmistakable."

"The evidence, dear Max, may be read a number of ways."

Oh, you insufferable scientist! I thought. *You objective ninny! Why can't you have the heart of a zealot?*

On another occasion, Darwin spoke to me of his awe at the sheer number of differing creatures he had come across on this journey. The implication in his voice was that God had done some mighty fancy things. I had another idea.

"Why would God make so *much* of it?" I asked. "I mean to say, there is a lot here that we could certainly do without."

Darwin shrugged. "I suppose He knew what He was doing."

"Suppose, do you? Well, suppose you suppose incorrectly?"

"We shall all know, some day."

"In the great by and by?"

"In the great by and by."

"No such thing."

"Oh, Max, you are so serious." And he smiled. But I detected the slightest discomfort in that smile, as if I were suggesting thoughts he himself harbored, yet shuddered to unloose.

Such signs from young Darwin gave me hope, even though he believed in a Creator, as he told me on several occasions. In fact, I pushed him so far one day that he stamped his foot. "Max!" he protested. "God exists, and I'll hear no more about it!" And he stormed off.

Was I daunted by this? No. I knew the heart of man because I knew my own heart. I knew that evil dwelt inside us all. I knew that a man could change for the worse. I vowed to pursue young Darwin, much as Darwin pursued his bugs.

We had, after all, several more years to go on the voyage.

XI

FitzRoy was suspicious of me, of course. He was a devout Christian. I detested him.

He and Darwin mixed it up once on the subject of slavery. FitzRoy was for it, Darwin against it.

I laugh now when I think about it. Darwin against slavery, yet his theory justifies slavery quite nicely. The strongest survive. Might makes right.

So slavery is a child of evolutionism. If we are all biological accidents, why shouldn't the white accidents own and sell the black accidents?

We arrived at the Galapagos Islands in 1835, a God forsaken (you'll pardon the expression) piece of the world 650 miles off the coast of Ecuador. Thirteen big and a number of small islands, just sitting there in the ocean.

This archipelago was as inviting as a stove. What was the point of stopping here? These islands were nothing more than piles of lava, with very little vegetation. The only thing worth noticing, if you want to call it that, were the strange creatures crawling over the crusty surfaces. Giant iguanas, monsters tucked inside bags of wrinkled skin. Oversized tortoises, whose function in the world I could not understand. Flightless cormorants, with their long necks, webbed feet, and hooked beaks.

Such ugliness!

Did Darwin agree with me? Of course not. The knothead was absolutely fascinated. What does one do with a knothead? Hope to unravel the knot, that's what. But Darwin's knot was tight.

Then, one day, the first thread came loose.

I was relaxing with a pipe on deck when Darwin approached me looking concerned. His usual enthusiasm was missing.

"I've noticed something curious," he said.

"Everything is curious to you."

"But this is very curious. Very curious indeed."

I leaned back and blew a puff of pollutant into the sea air. I knew I didn't have to respond. He would tell me. He always did.

"There are hundreds of islands in these parts," he said.

"Curious indeed," I answered.

"That's not the curious part, Max."

"Oh?"

"No, the curious part is this. Most of the islands have similar life forms on them. Birds, reptiles, and the like."

"Bravo for the islands."

"Yet, on these differing islands, you find that the creatures have marginal variations which differentiate them from their fellows on another island. In the finches, for example. I've noticed it especially in the finches."

Again, I puffed. Dolt that I was, I couldn't see where this was leading. Darwin paused in his narration and looked reflectively at the horizon. His brow furrowed. I always responded well to a furrowed brow. It meant a man was vulnerable.

"So?" I asked.

Darwin looked back at me. "So this. Seeing such a diversity of structure in one small, intimately related group of birds, one might really fancy that from an original paucity of birds in these islands, one species had been taken and modified for different ends."

The sentence struck me, though I wasn't sure of the point. Something, however, told me to remember those words. In a moment, I would know why.

"Who or what took and modified these birds?" I said, sitting up.

"That appears to be the question, as Hamlet might say."

"Are you saying it was your Creator God?" I tried to make the words pregnant with contempt.

"That's just it, Max. I wonder what God's purpose would be in making such slight variations. I can think of none."

"So that leaves you with what?" I asked anxiously.

"With some other force at work. A purely natural force, operating entirely out of God's direction. A blind, yet selective, force. Strange."

This is it! I thought. *The moment is here! Strike, Max, strike!* "Blind force, you say? Out of God's direction? Or, perhaps, there is no God."

The naturalist shuffled his feet. "I wouldn't go that far, Max."

"And why not? If the evidence suggests such a thing, aren't you bound to follow it?"

"The evidence is inconclusive."

"It is as plain as the nose on your face!"

Darwin frowned mightily and said, "Max, you are the devil from hell!"

To which I replied, "Even the devil from hell may speak the truth!"

"No, Max, no!" Darwin turned and almost ran away from me, as if to spend another moment in my presence would have meant some awful consequence. Yes, a consequence so grave and shattering that it could not be faced.

Suddenly, I laughed. And I kept on laughing. I could not stop myself. I laughed and stumbled to the bow of the ship, now pointing toward the darkening horizon.

Looking up into the night sky, I raised my fist and shouted: "I shall have Him now! You shall not have Him! I shall have Him and with Him the world! Try to stop me! Just try to stop me!"

No answer to the challenge came from the black clouds.

I took that as a good sign.

XII

For the rest of our journey—around the Horn to Australia, to the Cape of Good Hope and thence back to England—I did not let a single day pass without making some sort of suggestion to the increasingly uncomfortable naturalist of the *Beagle*.

"Is it not amazing, Chuck (I had taken to calling him Chuck), that the world holds such abundant evidence of natural changes in the species?"

"You are assuming a great deal, Max."

"Am I? I was just checking."

"Were you? Is that all?"

"I think man in general is ready for a change from outmoded conceptions of God."

"Outmoded? God can never be outmoded."

"Depends, Chuck. Who would have thought finches would differentiate on different islands? Doesn't seem like they needed much help from a God!"

"That's jumping to conclusions."

"Jumping? Or merely stepping?"

"I'm not going to stand here bandying fine points of syntax with you."

"Chuck, think of the wonders that lie ahead of you, as you dig and dig and classify and analyze. It's as if tens of thousands of years have left their history in the earth's crust."

"There is much to discover."

"Hmm. I wonder why our supposed Creator did not reveal all this to us. Eh?"

"Are you impugning God's wisdom?"

"Is there a God?"

"Max, please!"

"My father was a swine, Chuck."

"Really?"

"Yes. Intolerant, without any redeeming human traits. I don't think a loving God would have allowed him to be my father."

"The ways of God are beyond us much of the time."

"That so? Your father tell you that?"

"He wants me to be a clergyman."

"Wouldn't that be His final revenge? Making you in His image and not allowing yours to flourish."

"I wish you wouldn't speak of Father that way."

"Does the truth have a sting?"

"Leave me alone, Max!"

And so forth. I was planting seeds in the fresh soil of Darwin's fertile mind. My five years with Darwin convinced me that it would be a long and arduous project to make of him an atheist. But I was fueled with hope, somehow. This nascent doctrine of evolution seemed the key to everything. My sights were set on Darwin, but also beyond.

To the whole world? I shuddered with delight every time I thought about it.

As the *Beagle* set sail for home, for England, I had cause to rejoice. The voyage had not produced anything, so far as I could tell, that confirmed the existence of God,[4] Captain FitzRoy's Christian poppycock notwithstanding.

Down at the station, I happened by none other than Joel Nairobi, who was getting the third degree from a bull behind a desk. When Nairobi saw me his eyes went wild. "Keep him away from me!"

"What's the problem?" the officer asked.

"Yes, Mr. Nairobi," I said, "what is the problem?"

Nairobi squirmed in his seat. "I have nothing to say to you."

"Nothing? After all we've been through?" I said.

"Our private conversations, Mr. Bell, are such that I am not anxious to continue with them."

Then I got a sudden, crazy thought. Quickly I said, "Then I guess I'll be forced to swear out a complaint."

"Forced?" Nairobi said.

The officer glared at me.

"Mr. Nairobi and I were about to undertake a business transaction. I thought we might still be able to, but if he won't talk to me, then we'll be forced into a victim-perpetrator relationship, and that always makes for bad business."

Nairobi quickly shrugged his shoulders, "Well, talking perhaps..."

Dundy stomped over. "What's this all about?" he demanded.

"Who knows?" the officer grunted.

Dundy stood toe to toe with me. "Talk to me, Bell."

"Mr. Nairobi, my business partner, will be happy to supply you with my whereabouts at the time of the murder."

As the words left my mouth I wondered if I'd overestimated Joel Nairobi's ability to think quickly. I got my answer when Nairobi said, "Yes, Lieutenant, you see we were discussing business together, certain matters at Mr. Bell's office."

So there I had it—a solid alibi that would leave Dundy no choice but to let me go, and leverage over Joel Nairobi. Maybe I could use that leverage to get to the bottom of things.

"You think you're pretty cute, don't you?" Dundy said.

"Not cute enough to make it on the cover of *GQ*," I said, "but maybe just enough to get a Writ of *Coram Nobis* if I don't get my manuscript returned to me by the close of business today."

Dundy squinted. It was the squint of a cop who was face to face with his worst nightmare—a lawyer who knew a legal maneuver that could cause him great embarrassment. "Just have a seat," Dundy said finally. "I'll see what I can do."

I'm glad he didn't go check the books, as I wasn't sure what a Writ of *Coram Nobis* was. It was just a name I remembered from my English Common Law class.

The officer questioning Nairobi, with evident disgust, told him to "get lost." Nodding primly, Nairobi began putting on his gloves as the officer pounded off toward the coffee maker.

"An expression of, shall we say, thanks is in order," Nairobi said.

I said, "Save it. Just answer me one question."

"Yes?"

"Is the opera over?"

A look of confusion rippled across his dark face. "What opera?" he said. "*Phantom?*"

"Nevermind. Just remember I have something you want. And now I want something."

"And that is?"

"I want to know who your boss is. I want to talk to her myself."

"I will consider your request, Mr. Bell, but for now, good night." With that, the Moroccan bowed and scooted out the door. Dundy kept me waiting another half hour. I didn't like the look on his face when he returned. "I, uh..." he began.

"Yes?"

"We can't find it."

"You *what!*"

"You heard me!"

"You're telling me it's missing?"

Dundy shuffled his feet and hitched his pants. They immediately fell again under his ample waistline. "That's what I'm telling you."

I ran my fingers through my hair. "Does the word *negligence* mean anything to you?"

"Don't push your luck, Bell."

"I'm pushing. I want a full investigation of this, starting *now,* or I'll pay a little visit to my city beat friend at the *Times.*"

"Don't worry, will ya? Just give me a statement about the Hinkle murder and you can be on your way."

Forty minutes later I emerged from the building. The sun was setting on the city of angels, casting a pale orange hue over the skyline. I had one more call to make before I hunkered down to figure out how to get the Busby manuscript back.

Chaz was on old shoeshine guy down on Temple Street, just outside the Hall of Administration. My Dad had known him back when Dad was practicing in the criminal courts. Chaz was a "secret" a few of us knew about.

"Why, Mr. James Scott Bell," Chaz beamed as I took a seat. "Long time no buff!"

"Give 'em a special, Chaz. I want to comb my hair by 'em."

"I'll make 'em shine like Willard Scott's head." Chaz pulled out a can of polish and set about his work. I took a quick look around and leaned over to whisper. "A professor was murdered over at UCLA today."

Chaz didn't look up. "Uh-huh. A student upset with his grade?"

"Nope. Looks professional."

"I'm listenin'."

"His dying words were, 'The opera is over.' What do you make of that?"

"My hearing isn't so good," Chaz said, slapping on more polish. I smiled, pulled a five out of my pocket, and slipped it into his hand. "That's one ear," Chaz said, "but the other one's still plugged up."

I grunted as I handed him another five. "Price has gone up since Dad practiced law," I said.

"Inflation," said Chaz.

"So?"

Chaz chortled. "Mr. James Scott Bell, were you born stupid, or did you have to work at it?"

"Come on, Chaz!"

"Easiest ten bucks I ever made. Listen to me now. The opera ain't over till the fat lady sings. Ever heard that?"

Of course! It was obvious. Obvious now that I'd paid for the most expensive shoeshine in L.A.

"So if you were a betting man," I said, "you'd put money down that a fat lady was involved in this somehow."

"I'm sorry, my ears are getting clogged again."

"Yeah, well you'll have to see a doctor. Finish the shoes."

He did, with one big smile on his face.

It was dark now, and my car was still parked at the university. I went to a phone booth to call a cab. My second dime had barely dropped when I felt the barrel of a gun in my spine. "Don't move," a soft voice said. "Somebody wants to see you."

XIII

Upon our return, Darwin took up residence in London.

What was I to do? As far as Darwin was concerned, our association was at an end. He had things to do, speeches to give, journals to write. What further need had he of me?

I had to find some way to ingratiate myself to Darwin anew.

After some investigation, I determined that my notoriety with the police had waned in the five years I'd been at sea. I had by this time grown a large beard, and so I now felt sufficiently disguised to begin a new life as Max Busby, intellectual raconteur.

I joined the Geological Society of London, being accepted in part because of my association with Darwin aboard the *Beagle*. I knew that Darwin would be speaking frequently here.

It was at one such address that I "bumped into" him.

"Chuck, my lad! How good to see you."

"Well hello, Max." He seemed neither warm nor hostile. "Are you a member here?"

"Why yes. You know, Chuck, it was your influence over these last five years that has led me here. I am now so interested in the subjects you spoke of, I am dedicating my life to their pursuit."

His eyes widened a bit. "I influenced you?" he said.

"Of course."

"And here I thought you were trying to influence me!"

"Now what on earth gave you that idea?"

And that was good enough for Darwin. I made sure to see him often after that, to discuss geology and biology, and generally to make myself one of his circle.

This proved profitable. Virtually all of his friends were, to one degree or another, prompting him further and further along the pathway of natural science. But there was one person who was a stumbling block. One person who became the object of my hatred and revulsion. One person who almost ruined the whole plan!

Emma.

Emma Wedgwood, the woman Darwin married. He could not have made a more ill advised decision. She was a Christian.

Oh, how Christians became a thorn in my side! I shall never forget the feelings that swirled inside me one Autumn day in 1838. I was walking along Regent Street when I heard someone calling my name. Turning, I saw Darwin running excitedly toward me.

"Max, I have it!" he cried.

"Have what?"

"The answer. Look." He produced a sheaf of pages from his coat pocket and shoved them into my hands. "Just read the first paragraph."

I did so. It read: "Selection is the keystone of man's success in making useful races of animals and plants. But how does selection apply to organisms living in a state of nature? In the struggle for existence, it must be that favorable variations tend to be preserved and unfavorable ones destroyed. The result of this is the formation of a new species."

I looked up at Darwin. "By golly, that's it!"

"Yes! I know from Lyell that changes in the earth take place over great expanses of time, tens of thousands, perhaps millions of years."

"Millions? Are you mad?"

"Why not? Once you get beyond the seven-day theory, the door is open."

Music to my ears! Darwin had rejected a literal reading of the first chapter of Genesis!

"Chuck, you must publish this at once." I thought my encouraging tone would garner an immediate agreement. But his face turned dark.

"No, Max. I will not publish this."

Incredulous, I shouted, "Why on earth not?"

"It would hurt Emma," he said.

That woman!

"And besides, Max," he said, now much subdued and anxious, "if what I say here is true, my conception of God would have to change radically, if you know what I mean."

I did indeed. Darwin was caught in a classic inner struggle between two personalities. First, his very self, raised in the faith, a believer in God, and second, his objective investigative self, which was pointing him away from the former.

And I was determined that his latter self should win. No matter the cost. Even in lives.

XIV

The years wore on. And Charles Darwin, due almost entirely to my prodding, kept on writing. Finally, in 1844,[5] he had the rough draft of a book which described the theory of evolution.

The day after completing it, Darwin invited me over to Down House, his residence in Kent, sat me in a chair, and asked me to read. I did so, during which time Darwin paced nervously in the garden.

What I read was revolutionary. What I read was astounding. What I read would change the earth forever, if it was accepted. The gears were meshing, and I was the machinist.

The gist of Darwin's argument was as follows:

Animals of the same species varied. These variations were passed down from one generation to another. Eventually, enough of a difference was manifested to call the new group a new species.

In other words, the varieties *within* a species and those *between* species were only a matter of magnitude. Species did not differ in essence, only in the extremity of their variations.

In the breeding of animals, man was able to produce more favorable variations within a species. Darwin argued that, in nature, a selection process also took place during the struggle for survival. Favorable variations would conquer. In this competitive world, animals would tend to find favorable niches to occupy. Also, geological changes would produce different physical locations.

Let this happen for a significant period of time, thousands of generations, and you will produce new species.

That, at least, was the theory.

Darwin acknowledged it had weaknesses. He didn't know, for example, what produced the variations in the first place. Another flaw was the apparent lack of transitional forms in the fossil record. We should have expected to find myriad transitions but in fact found precisely the opposite. Species appeared fully distinct.[6]

But these matters could await further study.

The main point was, this theory completely undermined the need for a supernatural force to account for us. We were, according to the theory, happy, sentient accidents of blind nature. I even began to believe it myself.

I ran out to the garden.

"This is it, Chuck," I exclaimed. "There is no excuse not to publish it now."

He looked at me sadly. "You know what this is like?" he said. "It's like confessing a murder."

How apt. It was indeed like confessing a murder, the murder of the Almighty; the death knell of the Church. I saw it as a time of celebration; Darwin was preparing to mourn.

"I will not publish it, Max," he said.

I made no attempt to retain my temper. "You fool, you simpleton! You have spent years on this theory, and now that it is ready you plan to keep it to yourself? What is going on inside that head of yours?"

"Headaches," he said.

"Headaches?"

"I have been taken ill, Max, these last few months. I can't seem to shake it. I get constant headaches, stomach pains, and fatigue. I can only conclude it is related to my theory. Every time I think about it, I get sick."[7]

"It must be because you know, inside, you must publish it. Your body is rebelling against your delay."

Sadly, he said, "No, Max. I fear it is the opposite."

"What do you mean by that?"

He didn't tell me. Instead, making the excuse that he had to rest, he bid me good day.

It was not a good day, and I was not going to quit.

I made my way around to the side entrance and, undetected, entered the house. I don't know what I was looking for. But I didn't have anything to lose, either.

I heard voices from the library. I tiptoed to the door, and listened.

Darwin was talking to his wife in a tired voice.

"Might this not be God's warning to you, dear?" Emma said. "Might you not be struggling against the true order of the universe?"

"Oh, Emma. What shall I do?"

"Nothing," Emma said. "You must not do anything."

Wench! I thought.

"But all these years of work, of brooding."

"Dear, would it make it any better to make public your speculations? Would the publication of error be wise?"

"But that's just the point, Emma darling. I wouldn't be considering publishing it if I thought it was error."

"We've had this conversation before, dear. You may be wrong, and then you have made a terrible mistake."

"But I may be right as well." Now his voice sounded positively desperate.

"Now, now, you rest," Emma said. "And forget all about publishing right now. Take up your barnacles again. That will relax you. You can always change your mind down the road."

"You take care of me, don't you, dear?"

I'll take care of her, I thought.

"I love you, Charles. And because I do, I must make one further recommendation."

"Yes, dear?"

"Do you think it wise to give an ear to zealots?"

"Such as?"

Such as?

"Such as Max Busby. He is so violently against God."

Perceptive woman.

Darwin said, "Max is sincere, I think. Yes, he is an avowed atheist, but he has shown me such support over the years."

"I fear his influence on you," Emma said.

"Don't fear, darling. I won't publish the thing. I'll get back to my barnacles, and maybe back to my health."

"Thank you, dear. That's what I wanted to hear." She paused. "What was that?"

I had grunted involuntarily, my fuming insides belching flame up through my throat. I tiptoed like crazy back to the side entrance, and out into freedom.

XV

I collared Lyell at the Society.

"Our boy is collapsing," I said, as ominously as I could. "We must bring all our influence to bear on him."

"What do you mean collapsing?" Lyell asked.

"I mean, he's going balmy trying to decide whether to publish his theory. It's essentially complete."

Lyell assured me he would speak to Darwin. He also told me another one to contact, someone who was a very persuasive advocate, who had met Darwin, and who might be the one to push him to publication. The man's name was Thomas Huxley.

XVI

Professor Thomas H. Huxley was a bulldog of a man, with large mutton chop sideburns and a clear, resonant voice. He did not believe in the Almighty. I liked him immediately.

We met at an ale house in London. It was at that meeting that the Darwin conspiracy began.

Huxley represented the new order of things. Here was a purely naturalistic man, and violently so. He was a man for modern times. The air was rife with revolution, all over the globe—for certain we knew of one brewing in Paris as well as in central Europe. Marx had finally published his *Communist Manifesto*. People seemed poised, ready for new ideas.

Progress was on the march, like a mighty army. But like any mighty army, it was not without an enemy.

That enemy was the Church.

The Church stood for death. It upheld the God I wanted to kill.

I tried to make this clear to Huxley during our first meeting.

He was intrigued. "I have not thought about it in quite these terms before," he said.

"But it is so, is it not? Ever since Copernicus, the Church has been at war with we men of science."

"I have viewed it more as simple lagging. You do, however, seem to have a point."

"If we do not press an attack, Professor, we will be pushed into the mire. It is war."

Huxley pondered this a long while.

I said, "I see a two step operation which must take place. First, Darwin must be convinced to publish his theory. But second, and most important, we must push the consequences of that theory in the court of public opinion. Darwin, I'm afraid, is not the one for the job. Judging from his current disposition, his heart would not be in it."

Huxley nodded forcefully and raised his glass. "I will happily debate the merits of Darwin's theory, if he should ever choose to publish them," he said.

And so it began. Thomas Huxley was the man for the great task of destroying the Church in the crucible of public discourse.[8]

XVII

Unfortunately for me, Darwin did not relent. He was content to fiddle with his blasted barnacles. All the influence of Huxley, Lyell, Hooker and others could not sway him.

I was sure it was Emma who held him back.

The inner struggle did not abate in Darwin, apparently, for he was often ill, and on several occasions could not see me.

But his stubborn refusal was getting ridiculous. I feared the world would never hear of Charles Darwin. And worse, someone might beat him to the task, someone over whom I held no influence.

Alfred Russell Wallace, a naturalist fourteen years Darwin's junior, had remarkably been working on a theory similar to Chuck's.

Wallace was living and researching in Indonesia. He had an idea about the origin of species but was unable to offer a theory on how it happened. Then, in 1858, he fell ill with a bout of malaria. It was in this condition that Wallace, quite independent of Darwin, hit upon the idea of natural selection.

Having met Darwin previously, at which time they discussed evolution, Wallace was eager to have Darwin's opinion on his sudden insight. He quickly wrote out the essentials of his argument and sent the letter to Darwin.

Darwin was crushed. He summoned Lyell and myself to Down House and, quite despairing, showed us Wallace's letter.

"What shall I do?" Darwin said mournfully. "Wallace says nothing about publication. But as I had not intended to publish anything, can I do so now, honorably, just to usurp Wallace's priority?"

"Why not?" I said.

"It would be a paltry thing to do."

Cursed honor! Darwin, having not yet consigned God to the trash heap of history, was still fully within His ethical grasp. "Paltry pish posh," I sputtered. "You're the one who has labored so long on this theory. Now this young upstart comes upon it in a twinkling of an eye, and you are not prepared to take your rightful place in history?"

Darwin said, "I must do what is right."

"But who tells you what is right?"

"What do you mean, Max?"

"I mean, if we are indeed creatures who have evolved from lower life forms, which have no ethical capacity, are we not free also to evolve our own ethical system?"

Lyell said, "He has a point, Charles."

Darwin shook his head. "Same old Max. Still trying to convince me we can do without God?"

"Chuck," I said, "it's the logical consequence of your findings. When will you accept it?"

I could see Emma glaring at me from the hall. I glared back.

Darwin said, "I have a headache."

Lyell and I left without having secured Darwin's pledge to publish. Lyell waved his walking stick as he spoke. "This is a terrible occurrence. Wallace will surely take Charles' rightful place. Max, you always have ideas on strategic matters. What shall we do?"

"We need at least his permission to present his ideas, perhaps before the Linnean Society. We can convince him that we will also publicize Wallace's views along with his, but that we can skew the readings toward Chuck."

"Will he allow that? You know him well."

That was the rub. Darwin was still entangled in the web of Christianity. He did have his doubts, now grown strong over the years of brooding on evolution, coupled with my unrelenting atheistic suggestions. But he had not yet broken free. My fear was, if he did not make the break soon, Emma would keep him firmly within a faith, however fragile it might be.

But then, as it had in the past, fate took a hand—with poor Darwin's son.

XVIII

Like a shark attacking where blood is loosed, I sank my teeth into Darwin, and ate up the last of his faith.

The death of little Charles Waring Darwin from scarlet fever came at the perfect time for the conspiracy. Within days, I was at Down House, purportedly to comfort the grieving Darwin. But I had other plans.

"Cursed providence, old man," I said.

"Oh Max, Max," Darwin moaned.

"But God's ways are mysterious, I suppose."

"Don't speak to me of mysteries now, Max."

"I was speaking rather of God."

"Why?"

"Wondering how He can allow such an evil thing to happen."

"Max, please."

"I suppose we must have faith, is that it?"

"Don't, Max."

"Faith that when an innocent baby dies, by disease or the sword, we are to accept that as part of a greater purpose."

Darwin was silent. I continued, "And all the suffering, too, the crying of the hungry infants, the shrieking of the maimed, these are all signs of God's control."

I spoke softly and saw no need to embellish. Darwin was trembling in his chair.

"Oh, Chuck, I am sorry," I lied. "How ghastly of me to ramble on about my personal beliefs at a time like this. Do forgive me, old chap." I patted Darwin's knee. "Let me relieve you of some of the burden you must be feeling. Lyell and I have thought of a way to take the pressure off you on this Wallace development."

He looked up, the faintest glimmer of hope in his dark eyes. "How so?"

"Allow us to present both views at the Linnean Society. Lyell will set it up. You don't have to take any part in it. You don't have to risk any honor. With this most recent unfortunate circumstance, everyone will quite understand."

At that point, Emma appeared. Her moon face was as cold as the lunar surface itself. "He's had enough for today," she said.

I stood. "What say you, Chuck?"

"I said that's enough," said Emma.

"Emma dear, it's all right. Max is trying to help."

"It's about the theory, isn't it?" Emma said, insightful girl that she was. "What is dear Max proposing?" She said "dear Max" as if it were a disease.

"He and Lyell will be responsible for its presentation. I'll just stay in the background."

"No," Emma said. "I can't allow it. It's too sudden and follows too soon on our tragedy. It can't be God's will."

That's when it happened. Darwin stood and faced his wife, and in the most reproachful tone I had ever heard from his lips said, "I can't see where God has anything to do with anything. Max and Lyell shall have it!"

Emma's face darkened. The shadows of shattered faith fell over her. It was too much. She turned and, weeping, left the room.

I can only speculate on the momentous feelings that must have coursed through Darwin's soul at that moment. Sorrow, a bit of self-loathing perhaps, but at the same time a catharsis, a freedom, a breakthrough he had sought ever since his days on the *Beagle*. It is no easy thing for a man to renounce beliefs he has held all his life. But that is what had finally happened.

Charles Darwin, at least for all practical purposes, was now an atheist.

I had won him at last!

XIX

July 1, 1858.

We presented the idea of natural selection to the Linnean Society, giving Darwin the lion's share of the credit. Then we sat back and awaited the plaudits of the scientific community.

But the plaudits never came.

Apparently, the scientific community wanted evidence.[9]

Darwin had pledged to begin putting together a massive text on the subject. This would be the work of years, however. And now, suddenly, there was a need for something immediately. The big book would have to wait. Lyell and I pressed Darwin to slap something together for the interim.

And that is how Darwin's most famous book came about. I had suggested a title, *On the Non-Necessity of a Creator*, which both Darwin and Lyell rejected. Instead, Darwin called it *On the Origin of Species by means of Natural Selection, or the Preservation of Favoured Races in the Struggle for Life*.

You couldn't dance to it, but it did the job.

It was published on November 24, 1859, and the first edition sold out that same day.

We had a bestseller on our hands.[10]

XX

One thing bothered me a great deal about the book. It was the last paragraph. Emma's influence, I am sure. Darwin concluded his text with these words: "From the war of nature, from famine and death, the most exalted object which we are capable of conceiving, namely, the production of the higher animals, directly follows. There is grandeur in this view of life, with its several powers, having been originally breathed by the Creator into a few forms or into one; and that, whilst this planet has gone cycling on according to the fixed law of gravity, from so simple a beginning endless forms most beautiful and most wonderful have been and are being evolved."

Creator! He was still hanging onto the last vestiges of moribund faith!

I was furious, but gradually my fury subsided. For I realized it was no longer Darwin who mattered, but the theory. It was out now and, like one of Pandora's evils, it was in the world to stay.

XXI

The species hit the fan, as they say.

Huxley and I had prepared for it, knowing that faith and science would become locked in a mortal combat. We had to start at once to seize the day.

A stroke of good fortune got us off to a rousing start.

The most important organ of public opinion in England was, of course, *The Times*. The assignment to review the *Origin* was given to a Mr. Lucas, who wasn't scientifically up to the task. He had to turn to an expert for help.

He turned to Huxley.

We worked on the review together, skillfully blending objectivity with praise, so the result would be a seemingly fair minded appraisal.

Fair minded? Who wanted that? All we wanted was to win.

Huxley, to be perfectly honest, had a few doubts about Darwin's theory, in particular the transitional difficulty. Rather than transitional forms, Huxley saw sudden "jumps" in the fossil record. But I made sure to dampen those doubts whenever I could, convincing Huxley that the fight must be joined, and the enemy subdued.

That enemy, the Church, was in fact about to lose its first major skirmish on the evolution question.

It would not be its only loss.

XXII

Before what would come to be known as "The Great Debate," I'd found some success convincing certain clergymen to hop aboard the Darwin express. I knew that infiltration of the Church was a necessary prong of my overall plan.

The idea was to get Darwin preached from the pulpit without revealing the logical outcome of such a position—that is, the evisceration of Genesis and from there, on a slippery slope, the entire practical authority of the Bible. Inevitably, that outcome would be a natural result down the line if only evolution were first adopted.

It was like planting the germ of a virus. Sickness and death would come later.

Thus, when the well regarded Reverend F. J. A. Hort swallowed *Origin of Species* hook, line, and finches, I was gratified beyond words. In a letter to a friend, he wrote in exactly the terms I had anticipated: "My feeling is strong that the theory is unanswerable. If so, it opens up a new period in—I know not what."[11]

Precisely. Keep "what" hidden for right now.

But the Church as a whole was doing quite well in public opinion, and something had to be done about that. That is when the Great Debate fell into our laps.

In the summer subsequent to the publication of the *Origin*, the British Association for the Advancement of

Science held its annual meeting at Oxford. I learned that Dr. John W. Draper would deliver a paper discussing Darwin's theory. But that, in itself, was not so important. Far more significant was the news that Samuel Wilberforce, bishop of Oxford, would be in attendance.

Bishop Wilberforce, a florid and stentorian cleric known behind his back as "Soapy Sam," was a well-known opponent of Darwin's theory. He was also known for his mouth. He was attending, no doubt, in order to criticize the theory and defend the faith. Properly managed, I was certain we could turn this to our advantage.

Huxley was not so sure. "I'm not eager to give up an afternoon's peace and quiet in order to be episcopally pounded."

"But Hux, this is the moment we've been waiting for," I pleaded. "If you can do the pounding, it will be a major public victory."

"Yes, but how can I control the terms of the debate?"

"I have an idea."

"You always do," he said, and he listened as I proposed a most ingenious ploy.... .

XXIII

Bishop Wilberforce was eager to help a struggling pilgrim.

I sat in a chair in his study, and thanked him for seeing me. I made it appear that my words were a struggle to get out.

"I need help," I muttered.

"And just what is the matter, my son?"

"It's this Darwin business. It has produced a crisis of faith within me."

Wilberforce stared out the window. "Ah, my boy, you are not the first. This hateful doctrine is spreading like a toxin."

"If only there was something you could do to stop it!"

The cleric paused, as if deep in thought. When he glanced at me, I did my best to look pitiful and shaken. I widened my eyes like a beggar. He drummed his fingers on the cover of a large, worn Holy Bible.

"I will be attending the Association's presentation on this matter," he said presently. "I'll rise to speak at that time, and take on all comers. I cannot allow this to go on any further."

"Oh, that would be glorious!" I said. And then I dangled it before him: "In all of this, I think I should like to ask one of those Darwinists whether it was through my grandfather or my grandmother that I descended from a monkey." And I gave a half-hearted laugh.

The bishop, to my delight, laughed fully. "Oh, that's a good one," he said. "Quite good. Might even use that one myself some time."

"Oh feel free, my dear bishop, feel free!"

XXIV

The auditorium was filled to capacity, and a few of the attendees were snoring. Draper, giving the initial presentation, was a crushing bore.

But soon enough all would be wide awake.

Wilberforce sat in the east end of the gallery, with his small entourage. He had spotted Huxley sitting on the west side. He therefore knew that whatever he said would surely be countered by Huxley. That was exactly what I wanted him to know.

I sat rather in the middle, looking uncertain, and waved bravely to the bishop.

The bishop waved back. He was, of course, quite unaware that I had spent the previous evening drilling Huxley in preparation for the inevitable debate. Nor could he have known that I anticipated his use of my monkey ancestry remark at a critical point, and had, with Huxley, drafted a suitable reply.

You see, it was my view that public opinion would be molded by what I called a "bite," or catchy bit of jargon, rather than a fully thought-out argument.[12] The man on the street didn't seem to care about making relevant inquiries in detail. That was my strategy, at least. So get them talking on street level.

Draper, thankfully, finished in an hour, and the floor was thrown open. The bishop was recognized first.

Rising, he faced the august body and put on his best pulpit form. He waxed on about the need to assess, with objectivity and restraint, both the merits and demerits of any new idea. He attempted to do that with Darwin's theory, but with the limitation of a man who had been briefed on the idea, rather than having done the homework himself.

The bishop went on for perhaps twenty minutes.

And then he did it. Turning to Huxley whom, he acknowledged, was sure to forcefully reply, he said, "And pray tell, sir, is it through your grandfather or your grandmother that you claim your descent from a monkey?"

Looking satisfied, with a good-natured smile, the bishop sat.

Huxley whispered something to his neighbor, who happened to be the sergeant-surgeon to the queen. He told me later he had said, "The Lord hath delivered him into mine hands."[13]

One must understand the temper of the times to appreciate fully the impact of Huxley's next few words. We were still, in England, a people of the Church, bound to respect her even though her cultural walls were beginning to crumble. And clerics were treated with the utmost respect and dignity. It probably never occurred to Wilberforce that his offhand comment about grandparents would be handled the way Huxley handled it. No doubt the bishop had intended it as a somewhat good-natured stab, a little intellectual tease, which is exactly what I wanted him to intend.

The audience probably accepted it in that light as well. I noticed Lady Brewster with a smile on her face.

Huxley stood. All eyes were on him, all ears attuned. He did not smile. Instead, he looked the bishop directly in the eye and said, "I would rather be the offspring of two apes than be a man who was afraid to face the truth!"

A collective gasp arose from the assemblage. Then a scream. Lady Brewster had fainted.

The color drained from the bishop's face.

Insult a bishop? Such a thing was rare enough. But in public, in his own diocese? The shock waves would be immediate.

And that was our bite. It was all we needed. Huxley went on to defend the theory, but it was of no consequence. What the people would hear was that the Church had been characterized as foolish, anti-intellectual, obsolescent.

Evolution's conquest of the mind of man was off to a dandy start.

[Editor's Note: The Great Debate here described was a symbolic, as well as a substantive, watershed. The lines were clearly drawn, as Huxley wanted them to be. Church versus science. Old ways versus new. Superstition versus progress. And as we shall see, it was primarily "public relations" (rather than data and evidence) which cemented evolution in the popular mind. It still is, too. That point was recognized early on by the dark genius of Sir Max Busby.]

XXV

Of course, not all of science was ready to swallow Darwin's theory whole. Scientists were an odd lot, posing as coldly objective yet harboring passions and prejudices like any other pack of mortals. This was a fact that would serve me in good stead much later, when evolution was widely accepted. Once we got the majority of scientists to favor the view, a group dynamic would take over, and individual scientists would be loath to leave the flock, lest they appear foolish to their fellows.

But evolution by natural selection still had that major empirical flaw: the absence of transitional forms in the fossil record. This was hanging things up, to put it mildly.

I was able to convince Darwin, however, that science would come to a complete halt if theories had to wait for all the troubling pieces to fit into place. No, we should publish as much as we had, and claim that we expected time would provide the missing links.

Now, with things breaking fast and furious, we needed something bold and dramatic to "prove" our theory. News of the absence of transitional forms would be absolutely fatal.[14] What were we to do?

In my mind there was only one path to choose: deception.

But how? The key was the fossil record. If only we

could shore that up. Then the obvious plan presented itself. We would make a fossil forgery!

What we needed was some kind of transitional form, say between reptiles and birds. If we had that, Darwin's theory would be accepted forevermore!

During the first, furious weeks subsequent to publication of *Origin of Species,* I subtly interviewed interested parties for a position as co-conspirator (without their knowing it, of course). One of these people was a Dr. Haberlein, of Germany. He was a scientific dilettante, a collector, but most important, an opportunist. He came to England to find a way of cashing in on the coming evolution craze. I sized him up as a man who would make something up for money.

So I planted a suggestion in his mind.

"Wouldn't it be earth shattering," I mentioned casually one day as we sat at an outdoor cafe in the West End, "if a transitional form were dug up in a quarry somewhere? The timing is perfect."

"Such a thing would fetch a fair price, I'd wager," said Haberlein, sipping his sherry.

"It would be especially helpful if this thing were a transition between reptiles and birds. The feather question is a difficult one."

"How so?"

"There is nothing quite like a feather, you know. And to establish its intermediate form is a difficult proposition.

But suppose a fossil of small, reptilian bones were unearthed, along with the perfect imprint of an accompanying feather? What would you think of that?"

"A fair price," he said. "A very fair price."

"You know, a schoolboy could play quite a prank with this one." I laughed.

Haberlein didn't laugh.

I continued, "He could, this hypothetical schoolboy, take a paste concocted from powdered limestone and implant some small, ancient reptile bones in it, along with a feather. Instant fossil!"

Again I laughed. The power of suggestion is much more effective when the subject is not aware he is being "persuaded." Haberlein's eyes narrowed, and he appeared to be calculating something. We sat in silence for several minutes, and when next we spoke the subject was changed.

A few months later, Haberlein showed up in Munich with a most important slab of rock. A fossil it was, the imprint of some ancient sort of reptile. Only this one had a feather!

The stir this caused was widespread and instantaneous. The first solid fossil evidence that Darwin's theory was true! The scientific community went positively mad.

They got even madder at Haberlein. He kept trying to jack up the price for it, frustrating paleontologists and curators who lusted to own the thing. Haberlein played them like fish. He also gave a name to this "creature" immortalized by rock.

He called it *Archaeopteryx.*

Now, of course, all the way into 1926, *Archaeopteryx* was cited as the best evidence of evolution.[15]

XXVI

Deceptions would be important to my later work. I anticipated the Piltdown Man hoax and wanted to make ready any and all tactical advantages.

This is when I struck upon my most ambitious ploy.

To find the "missing link," or man in transition, would be the greatest discovery of all. My knowledge of the fossil record, coupled with my conviction that hoax was the only way evolution could be "proven a fact," of course ruled out an actual discovery. But what if a "man" were some day discovered, a race which formed a line of transition between ape and modern human?

At Music Hall one night, I saw an ingenious performer doing the "quick change" with costume and makeup. I went backstage and made his acquaintance. I also proposed a small job, which he was more than happy to take on, for a price.

We met at an artist's studio one Saturday morning. Through the wonder of makeup my upper body and face were given a dark, hairy, and primal appearance. And the artist I'd engaged made a woodcut of my "image."

I was the "missing link"! I had a picture now which I would someday produce, though I never did. I had no need. The theory caught on nicely without my ever having to publish it.[16]

[Editor's Note: With regard to the mythical "missing link," it is apparent to all now that the emergence of modern man was sudden, and represents a quantum leap over all alleged early hominids. In cranial capacity, vocal tract construction, and numerous other ways, modern man is not a descended species, but a distinct creation. Yet bone hunters eager for publicity continue to posit early ancestors for man. Finding a skull fragment from a large ape causes them to suspend their own cranial capacity and develop wild theories about bands of pre-men roving the African plane. Once again, though, the evidence simply isn't there. Sir Max knew this and posed for the woodcut as a result.]

XXVII

I next recruited a young German into the conspiracy.

Ernst Haeckel latched onto Darwinism with the zeal of a religious convert (which is what he was, of course). His attacks on Christianity in his home country were quite helpful.

Now our campaign could move to a new level. Under my direction, Haeckel expanded Darwinism beyond biology into a complete view of the world. Evolution meant progress, in every sphere of life. And that meant, of course, that God was not behind anything (the Germans were good for something after all).[17]

As effective as Haeckel was, another recruit, Wilhelm Bölsche, was even more so.

Could this chap write! And it was his writing, his poetic style, his way of capturing the imagination that was so deliciously effective. In his book, *Love-life in Nature: The Story of the Evolution of Love,* he wove Darwinism into a soft, warm, chewing gum religion that the lower classes could eagerly chomp:

And from the depths of the human soul, whence also the lessons of the gospels have come, still another voice whispers into my inner ear, a voice first heard in the wisdom of the ancient Indians. And it says that the band of community and

*brotherhood is not limited to man, but that it encompasses all
things on this earth, all things that grow up and evolve to their
peak under the sun's rays and in the silent grip of holy universal laws.*[18]

Ah, if only I could find someone like this for my next
target—America! That is where the real battle would be.
This upstart nation was beginning to assert itself in the
world, and I had the feeling that here the biggest battles
would be fought.

I couldn't have known then how right I was.

I was never able to develop an evolutionary poet like
Bölsche in America, which proved to be a detriment.[19]

But then, America offered other possibilities.

We walked down the hill, past City Hall, where a
car was waiting. The thug holding a gun in my
back was a kid, maybe twenty.

"Are we going to see her?" I said.

"Who?"

"The fat lady."

"Whatta you talkin' about?"

"She's your boss, isn't she?"

The kid stiffened and pushed the gun into my
rib cage.

There were two ways to play it—soft and compliant, or spit in the eye. For some reason just then I thought about Jesus, about the time Herod sent a Pharisee to him to tell Him to clear out of town. Jesus called Herod a fox (more like a "skunk" in those days) and said He wasn't about to clear out. That was "in the eye."

With a rush of adrenaline I said, "Your boss would love it if you plugged me, wouldn't she? Yeah, since I've got what she wants, that'd put you in solid."

"Get in!" the kid said. I hopped in the back seat of the sedan. The driver turned to me and smiled. It was Joel Nairobi.

"Now I've seen everything," I said. The kid, gun pointed at my chest, got in next to me.

"I assure you Mr. Bell," said Nairobi, "there is much left to see."

We headed down Wilshire.

"So you boys are in cahoots, eh?" I said.

Nairobi said, "I have found, Mr. Bell, that cahoots is a very profitable place to be."

"What sort of profit would that be, Joel?"

"Money, of course. What other profit is there?"

"I was thinking of the verse that says, 'For what shall it profit a man, if he shall gain the whole world, and lose his own soul?' You have a soul, don't you Joel?"

Nairobi was silent.

"I mean, fellas, when you die what's going to come of all that money? Do you think God is going to care that you played gangster?"

"I don't believe in God, Mr. Bell," Nairobi said.

"Why not?"

Nairobi shrugged his shoulders. "It seems rather senseless. We have evolution to account for life. What is there left for God to do?"

Chuckling, I said, "You mean you believe that chance mutation is the explanation for life as we know it?"

"I see no reason to discount the theory."

"But there's no solid proof, Joel."

"That is nonsense, sir."

"Take the kid here," I said. "Is he the product of mutation?"—I glanced at the kid—"Bad example. Let's take another one."

"Just keep it up," the kid growled.

"Do you know what the odds are against the basic enzymes of life arising from chance? About one in ten to the forty thousandth power. A mathematical impossibility. With those odds, I put my money on an intelligent designer. What do you think?"

"I think," said Nairobi, "that I am getting a headache."

"Maybe that's God calling you, Joel. And you, too, kid. Even you have a chance."

"Button it," the kid said.

The conversation effectively ended then as we pulled up to the Beverly Hilton Hotel. That was good luck for me. I knew the house detective. If he was around, I could play a hole card. I needed Nairobi to get to the fat lady, but I didn't need the kid and his gun. He was about to explode and I didn't want to be around when he did.

As Nairobi led me through the lobby, with the kid right behind, I saw Luke leaning on the concierge desk. I gave him a wave.

"Hello, Jim," he said, stepping over. Nairobi and the kid stopped in their tracks. The kid looked like he'd just bitten into a chili pepper on an acid stomach. "How's tricks?"

"Same. Hey, why do you let these cheap gunmen hang out in your lobby, with their guns bulging in their pockets?" I nodded toward the kid.

Luke gave him the up and down. "Well, if you don't want anything," he said, "beat it, and don't come back."

The kid's eyes widened. For a moment I thought he'd make a move. But Luke put his hand under his coat and pulled himself up to full authority. The kid looked at Luke, then around the lobby, then back at Luke and me.

"I won't forget you guys," he said, turning on his heels. I let out a sigh of relief. The kid trudged out the door as Nairobi shook his head.

"Got to go now, Luke," I said. "A date with a lady."

Luke nodded, then frowned. "Say, you're married, Jim. You're not that kind of guy."

Over my shoulder I said, "It's not that kind of date."

Nairobi had an elevator waiting for me. We got out on the fourth floor. Nairobi led me down the hall then stopped and gave a terse knock on a door. A lady opened it.

She was imposing, a hot air balloon with close-cropped, steel gray hair. She wore a sweater stretched to its Angora limits, and slacks made from the most elastic Spandex known to man. A permanent pout gnarled her face into a fist. She gestured us inside.

"So, Mr. Bell. We meet," she said, her voice a low rasp. Then to Nairobi: "Where's Wilmer?"

Nairobi said, "He, uh, was detained."

The fat lady's face grew tighter. "Just wait till I get my hands on him!"

"Who is this Wilmer?" I asked.

"He happens to be my son," said the fat lady, a coiled snake in her voice. "Sit down, Mr. Bell."

A tray of liquor sat on a small table by the divan. "Drink?" said the fat lady.

"Thanks...7-Up," I said.

Harrumphing, she poured me a 7-Up, and herself and Nairobi a bourbon. "Now let's get to it," she said. "I am Hillary Horton Malloy."

She waited for a response. "Congratulations," I said.

"You know who I am?"

"Sure. You're the second most famous atheist in America, after Madalyn Murray O'Hair."

Her entire body, at least what I could see of it, quivered into a grip of tension. She slammed her drink down on the table. "Don't *ever* mention that name in my presence again!"

In the awkward lull Nairobi said, "Mrs. Malloy is the more influential, Mr. Bell. When the history of this time is written, her name will appear ahead of that Texas impostor."

"One footnote canceling out another, eh?" I said.

"Enough!" Malloy said. "What do you know about my work?"

"Only that you are the bearer of the mantle of Lee Hubris Mellon, and that evolutionary theory is your favorite incendiary device. If we're to believe your press notices, you seek to usher the world into a bold new era of atheism. Am I close?"

"You've done your homework, Mr. Bell. And what do you think my chances are?"

"That depends."

"On what?"

"On whether Christians rise up to the challenge, and don't wimp out on this scientific stuff."

"Wimp out?"

"Sure, by sitting back and letting modern naturalistic science do all the defining. It's a world view you're pushing, and you're using science to foist a deception on modern man. How am I doing?"

She took a drink. "You're clever. Maybe too clever."

We sized each other up until Nairobi chimed, "Shouldn't we be getting, shall we say, down to business?"

"Precisely," Malloy said. "Do you have it?"

"No," I said. "But I can get it."

"And when you do, what price will you accept?"

"It's not for sale."

"I want that manuscript!" Malloy shouted. Her voice had an odd, hollow sound to it. "It is rightfully mine!"

"Right...fully?" I said slowly. My words were boulders being pushed through mud. The room began to spin.

I was aware of Malloy and Nairobi standing up, peering down at me. I looked at the floor. It became a blurry black hole. I dove in.

XXVIII

Another memory flashes. I am with a young man with a bushy mustache outside an Italian cafe. He is a philosopher, my favorite kind of animal, for philosophers are easily manipulated through logic and a touch of the bubbly.

The man is intense. His eyes keep darting about as if on the lookout for some universal truth trying to secretly whisk past his face.

When I slyly introduce the subject of "the Church," he goes wild. He begins to rant about Christianity as a crutch for the "weak herd."

When I hear that term, I bring up the name of Darwin. Isn't it true that Darwin's findings predict weaker and stronger "herds" among men?

The man nods vigorously.

I say there is almost a "natural aristocracy," almost a race of "supermen," which is inevitable in the Darwinian world. That is when the man's eyes sparkle like gas lights on a windy night! He pounds me on the back, as if to signal a gratitude of the highest magnitude. "I have broken through!" he shouts, neatly forgetting that it was I who made the suggestion in the first place.

He stands and quickly finishes his drink. As he storms off I call to him, asking his name.

"Nietzsche," he says, "Friedrich Nietzsche, the man who will engineer the death of God!"

A man after my own heart.[20]

XXIX

You, dear reader, may wonder why I never married. The answer is simple. I was a priest. All of my passions were directed toward my religious cause. What time had I for a wife, when I was busy with reversing the spin of the world?

What need had I of children, when the world I would leave to them would be a godless void of useless struggle? What desire had I to be a father, when my own was the devil from hell?

My focus was singular, and I was achieving success after success.

In 1880, I was knighted by the queen—no small feat for an atheist! But by that time I had learned to hide my philosophical persuasions in order to effect a greater "good."

It was a triumphant decade! Evolution had indeed woven itself into the imagination of Western Europe, and Russia was not far behind. I should have been the happiest atheist in all the world.

And yet...

One morning during this period of unrivaled achievement, I stood on the banks of the Thames and looked out at the fog rolling along the surface. The fog was a shroud, obscuring the crystalline waters, making hazy the outline of the buildings on the other side. This dark mist was a hindrance to pure sight. And I was mesmerized. For I realized something deep within me.

I was that fog.

Pure truth was what I was obscuring. I was rolling along over the surface of the world, my sole purpose that people should not see the truth.

Truth did not matter to me.

And then a thought like a thunderbolt rattled my mind: It did not matter to me that truth did not matter to me.

That thought filled me with an ineffable sadness. Upon what, then, was my life based? If not truth, what?

What?

Instantly the answer came to me—hate. Hate is what fueled my passions.

Well, hate is not exactly a balm from Gilead. I was filled with a sickness of soul that I scarcely recognized.

Suddenly up out of the London fog I seemed to hear a voice. I will not speculate upon the origins of it. I am not a mystic. But a voice indeed cried out from the fog, and it seemed to say "Turn back..."

Back? Back from what?

The voice simply whispered, "Turn back..."

Looking around, seeing no one, I addressed the fog itself. "What have you to do with me?"

"Turn back..."

"What are you talking about?" I demanded.

The voice grew faint. "Turn back...Turn back..."

I shuddered. The voice had begun to sound faintly familiar, as though emanating out of the shrouded mists of the past. And then it struck me that this voice was the one I least expected to hear.

It was the voice of my father!

Was I going mad? Was latent guilt over the murder of my own flesh and blood now welling up to torment me? Or could it be God playing a perverse trick, trying to capture my immortal soul, a soul I no longer believed in?

I rushed back to my flat. In a fit more becoming an inmate of Bedlam than a rational enemy of God, I began to tear the place apart.

"Silence!" I shouted to the voices in my head. Clothes and boots and bottles of cologne crashed in the four corners of my residence. Papers flew. I even unearthed a bundle long forgotten, one I had taken with me during the flight from my childhood village.

This bundle I threw across the room. It burst open, strewing knickknacks here and there, one of them falling at my feet. I stooped to pick it up.

It was a figurine, small and dark, crude in its way but unmistakably an angel.

"Willie," I whispered. And then I heard his voice, faintly murmuring from the distant past, "It'll protect you, I wager. Always."

I felt it again, the same warmth, the same infernal pull toward some source of goodness beyond the material world. It was as if I were being offered a choice. I could stop now, turn from my wicked ways, and find comfort where only true comfort resides.

"NO!" I screamed. "You shall not have me!" I shook my feeble fist at the ceiling. Pausing not a moment for thought, I stormed out to the London streets, down to the lower East End, where the pawnbrokers resided.

I picked the seediest looking one and charged inside. "How much?" I blurted. "How much will you give to relieve me of this ancient Greek masterpiece?"

The bearded thief behind the counter squinted at the angel. "Two pence," he said, "and not a farthing more."

"Done!" The price did not matter in the least. I only wanted to know that I had traded the one thing that seemed to offer hope, for a price. Like Judas Iscariot, I thought it only fitting. I wished now that it would end up in the hands of some other poor sinner, and vex him to near madness.

For several days I wandered the streets of London, like an escapee from the asylum at St. Mary of Bethlehem, forgetting to eat, to shave and generally growing to look myself like the missing link.

Voices! Distant memories! Angels! Demons! I was experiencing no less than a crisis of faith, evolutionary faith, and it was tearing me apart.

I think I should indeed have ended up in some lunatic bin, had it not been for a fortuitous bit of news.

XXX

Darwin was dying.

And that fact was doing something to his thinking. Rumor had it he was questioning his whole system, wondering if it was not all rather a house of cards.

Darwin had been my pawn, of course. But the frosting on the cake, as I viewed cake in those days, was his loss of faith. As long as Darwin remained a practical atheist, he was not a threat. Indeed, he had written *The Descent of Man,* an atheistic book if there ever was one.

But if Darwin were suddenly to return to the faith of his childhood, why, he might renounce his theory, and all my work would be lost!

Lost!

It was unthinkable. Incredible! I awoke from my slumbers and dove back into the fight. Never again would I question my cause or my commitment.

On my way to Down House one afternoon, I bumped into a Mrs. Philbert, returning from a visit there. She was an older woman, a widow, stout as a fire hydrant, and as capable of gushing a torrent of words as those municipal pressure caps can spew water. I therefore prepared to be verbally sprayed.

"Sir Max," she said. "How nice to see you!"

"Why Mrs. Philbert. How nice to be seen."

"Yes, quite…what? Well, never mind. You are on your way to Down House, I suppose?"

"Your powers of observation are as great as ever, I see." I chuckled good-naturedly. The humoring of widows was something I was good at.

"I wish the news were better," she said.

"Bad news?"

"Oh, yes. I'm afraid he's quite ill, quite ill. I don't think his heart will last."

"Lamentable," I said, trying to sound mournful. "A great man." Inside, I was smiling. The sooner death took Darwin, the better.

Mrs. Philbert pulled a kerchief from her purse and dabbed her eyes. "I can't help thinking that his theory is what killed him," she said.

"You mean, evolution?"

"The terrible pressure it has been on him these last weeks."

"What has happened these last weeks?"

"Aren't you aware?"

"No. Pray tell."

"And you, one of his closest and dearest friends!"

"Pray tell, I tell you!"

She continued, "Well, I don't have a mind for such things as science and such, but I have heard, in helping

Emma around the house, some of the discussion going on with the visitors. Naturally, their visits have been limited since his first attack—"

"Naturally."

"—it being a dreadful strain to go over and over these matters in the state of health he is in–"

"Yes, yes."

"—and him looking so pale—"

"Mrs. Philbert, the point?"

She straightened and looked as if she'd just awakened from a trance. "Oh, yes. I'm so sorry. Well, the long and short of it is, Sir Max, that Sir Charles is no longer sure about his theory being true, after all."

Cursed fate! There it was, the thing I had most feared. I would have dashed to Darwin's side then and there, had not Lady Chatterbox dropped another, more startling revelation.

"Of course," she said, "his eternal soul is my main concern. And for that, I have reason to hope."

Those words chilled me. "Hope? Why?"

She dabbed again, then said, "I think he is on the verge of embracing his Christian faith once again."

A knife to my heart would not have felt different to me. "Why do you say this?" The desperation in my voice again startled this bewildered widow.

"Grace," she stammered, "is a funny thing."

"Grace is a funny thing! This is your answer?"

"Why, Sir Max…"

"I ask you for a rational explanation, and all you can tell me is 'Grace is a funny thing'?"

She mumbled her next few words, an understandable reaction to the wildness in my eyes. "Well, I…that is, some have come to see him, including myself, to speak to him of his need for the Savior. He seemed to be listening."

"Blast!" I exploded, involuntarily.

"I beg your pardon?" she said, sounding quite shocked.

"Blest!" I said. "Blest he is to have such friends!"

"Oh," she said, and beamed.

"I really must hurry on to see him. Time is short." I began to edge away.

"I quite understand, Sir Max. You will be sure to speak to him of the Savior, won't you? Coming from you, it just might push him over the edge."

Almost at a trot now, I called back over my shoulder, "You can be sure I'll try to push him over the edge, Mrs. Philbert. You can be sure of that!"

XXXI

Darwin was resting in the garden.

I can't say Emma was glad to see me, but perhaps she believed it would revive her husband's spirits to see his oldest friend, one who went back to the *Beagle* days, and she led me to him. He did seem glad. Emma left us, after I promised not to cause any major excitements.

One should never accept a promise from a murderous atheist.

Darwin and I began a slow stroll along the grounds.

"Chuck, you certainly do look chipper," I said.

"You were always a good liar, Max. It was easy for you."

"No conscience," I said. "Convenient for we products of evolution."

He did not smile, as I'd expected. Instead, his eyes became ineffably sad under his white, bushy eyebrows.

"Ah, Max, how easy it is for you to disbelieve. I have never been quite comfortable with my atheism. I wish it were not so. I am seventy-three years old, on the brink of death I think, and shudder on the edge of the abyss."

He paused at a rose, as red as fresh blood, and delicately stroked the petals. "Is this flower really the product of chance, Max?" he said.

"Given enough time, Chuck, anything can happen. You know that."

He didn't answer. His thoughts, it seemed, were off somewhere, thinking ahead, or perhaps back. Wherever they were, I wanted them right here where I could get my hands on them.

"Chuck, your theory is well on its way to conquering the world. Don't talk nonsense now."

"Nonsense, Max? I am a man of science. At least, that's what I thought I was. Isn't the test for truth something more than whether an idea conquers the world? Winning isn't everything, is it Max?"

"Winning is not everything," I said. "It's the only thing." That sounded nice. I made a mental note to jot it down.

"Truth is the only thing, Max. Have I served the truth?" Standing there, as frail as one of the flower petals he caressed, Darwin gazed up into the sky. "You know what the Bible says heaven is like?"

I answered immediately, "Yes, a bunch of angels eternally singing the same bloody song."

He ignored me. "It says it will be like a banquet, a great feast. Max, don't you long for such a thing?"

I did not like the turn this conversation was taking. We were strolling again, Darwin still seeming off on some cloud. "We chance beings should not long for what is not there," I said. "Chuck, is this really you talking? What are you thinking?"

"I am thinking," he said quietly, "of taking it all back."

So it was true! Charles Darwin was considering throwing his lot in with the God I hated, and tossing out the theory at the same time!

"I am astounded, Chuck," I said quickly. "I am astounded beyond words! That you would do such a thing, not only to yourself but to me! I have dedicated my life to spreading your work to the world, my life I tell you! And you have the temerity to stand there and threaten to toss it aside like so much flotsam? I am at a loss, Chuck."

He listened, but his mood did not appear to change. "You're missing the point, old friend," he said. "This is not about feelings, this is about what really *is*. And I wonder how much we can ever really know. Are not some things beyond science?"

"Well, of course—"

"So there are things we don't know."

"I suppose so."

"Therefore, we cannot know *how much* we don't know. It may be more vast than the entire universe. The point is, Max, that something inside us cries out for meaning. Is that a feeling that has evolved? Can randomly made creatures seek things outside themselves? Or does the desire necessarily imply an object? And if that is so, does not our desire for heaven imply that such a thing exists?"

Now we were really heading for trouble. The cool rationality of his younger days was gone. There would be no reasoning with him, I was sure.

We walked on in silence, Darwin a little ahead of me. I noticed some cut branches the gardeners had left from their work earlier in the day. That's when it hit me, the thing I knew I must do.

I could not risk this metaphysical speculation to continue. Should Darwin confess his spiritual faith, as it seemed he was aiming to do, it would be big news. The churches would get hold of it and claim victory over the theory—evolution was false, after all. It would be a public relations disaster, and undoubtedly lead to some sort of religious revival.

The lengthening shadows of twilight had all but engulfed the garden at Down House. We were quite alone. There was no sign of Emma.

I silently picked up a tree branch.

Darwin's back was to me. He appeared to be studying the ivy that entwined the southern wall.

Slowly, I raised the branch. I held it out over Darwin's right shoulder. Simultaneously, I let the branch fall and shouted as loudly as I could, "BOO!"

His frail body quivered. His head turned and he saw the falling limb.

Eyes wide, his mouth sucked in a pathetic breath. Then he grabbed his chest, keeled over, and fell into a bush.

XXXII

Running to the house, I shouted, "Emma, Emma, come quick!" How was I to know the family doctor had just arrived? They both bolted out into the garden and found Darwin.

Alive, though barely.

The three of us managed to get him to his bed. The doctor, after a quick examination, did not look pleased. "You'd better make preparations, Emma," he said.

The old explorer's chest rose and fell weakly.

A bedside vigil began. Several friends, including the voluble Mrs. Philbert, and family members like daughter Henrietta, were there.

Darwin slept.

He awoke the next day. Several tried to speak to him, but he did not respond.

Finally, in the early afternoon, he looked as if he would speak.

As fate would have it, I was nearest the bed. I leaned over and Darwin whispered, "Max, I desire that feast in the sky." He reached up his hand toward me in an almost desperate gesture of longing.

"What? What did he say?" a few voices piped behind me.

Darwin had grabbed hold of my shirt. I quickly disengaged his hand, and patted it reassuringly, indicating with my facial expression that I would take care of it.

Quickly, I turned to the others in the room. "Outside please," I said, herding them with my arms, and the startled assemblage shuffled out the door.

We were in the hallway when Mrs. Philbert, her face crimson with excitement, said, "What did he say, what did he say? It sounded something like a 'feast in the sky.' What did he say, Max?"

"Ladies and gentlemen," I said calmly. "Sir Charles just told me this: 'I am not in the least afraid to die.' Perhaps now we ought to let him rest."

Mrs. Philbert's jowls wobbled, and likewise so did Emma's. The old girl insisted on rushing back to her husband's side. I tried to stop her, but she fought her way past me.

It did not matter, however, for when she entered the room, it was to make the discovery that Darwin was dead.[21]

I woke up in a dark, dank basement. No light made it through the window. My head felt like a soccer ball after a high scoring World Cup game.

There was no sound, except the distant honking of a truck horn as it passed by on what must have been a highway. Then I heard voices. They were muffled, but I could make out a few words:

"...fat lady...beat him up...get this over with... Geraldo won't like it."

Geraldo?

My mind reeled at the events of the last two days. I had been a happy attorney, minding my own business. Now, with a frightening suddenness, I was a prisoner and a pawn in some whirlwind game I knew nothing about.

I prayed for wisdom, courage, and strength. This was no time for modest requests.

There was only one door, and it wasn't one I wanted to try. A little window to the outside was boarded up, but maybe if I got my hand on it I could push my way through.

I took off my shirt and placed it over the glass. I whacked it with the heel of my shoe. That did the trick. Carefully, I removed shards of glass. Then I started to push against the old boards. They held fast. I needed to give a swift kick, but worried about the sound. Would that be enough for the goons in the next room to come in and "get this over with"?

I sent up a short prayer. "Lord, plug up the ears of the goons." I knew this probably would never make the Psalms, but it was short and to the point. I took a deep breath and pulled myself up onto the sill. Then I sent my left foot through the boards.

They gave, and made a sound like a short thunderclap. I paused a second, and didn't hear a reaction in the next room. A moment later I was in the light.

The house was in a rustic area, maybe Palmdale, about thirty minutes outside L.A. I ducked down a row of apple trees and ran for the road.

A semi was pulling out of a diesel station. I waved my thumb in his direction. He gave me the "come on" sign, and I pulled myself into the cab.

"Where you headed?" the driver—a lean, weathered man with a Kansas City Chiefs hat on—said.

"L.A."

"Big place. Where in L.A.?"

"Somewhere in the middle." I didn't want to go to my office. It was probably being watched. I needed time to think.

We rumbled down the 5 to 405, and the driver pulled off on Ventura Boulevard. He dumped me a block from DuPars, the famous flapjack restaurant in Studio City, and that's where I went.

I sat at the counter and felt in my pockets. I found three quarters. The waitress stood in front of me and scowled.

"Give me a cup of coffee and a doughnut, if that's enough."

The waitress stared at the lonely trio of coins I'd placed on the counter. "You want the coffee or the doughnut?" she said.

"Not both?"

"Not for that."

A voice from two stools down said, "Give him some ham and eggs." She was a sweet-faced girl, with long blonde hair, some of which looped over her right eye.

"That's nice of you," I said, "but I'm not hungry. A cup of coffee and a doughnut will fix me fine."

"Take ham and eggs. Might as well spend my last few bucks doing a good deed."

"Things a little tough, huh?"

"I'm not sitting here for local color. They locked me out of my room."

"Things are tough every place."

She moved to the stool next to me. "Drink your coffee while it's hot."

I said, "What did they lock you out of your room for?"

"Did I ask *you* any questions?"

"Sorry." I took a sip of coffee and said, "Been out here long? You trying to make it in show biz?"

"Something like that. I've had a couple auditions. I was up for a 'Married with Children.' "

"What happened?"

"They said I was too intelligent."

"Tough break."

"I was up for a 'Melrose Place,' too, but didn't get that one either."

"Maybe it's just as well."

"How come?"

"Have you ever seen 'Melrose Place'?"

"I'd take anything if they offered it."

"Doesn't sound like you're getting the breaks."

"My next act will be an impersonation of a young lady going home...on the thumb. Tell me *your* life story."

"Not much to tell. I'm in the middle of some international intrigue involving murder, mayhem, and a missing manuscript."

"Is that all?"

"For today."

She smiled.

"What's your name?" I asked.

"O'Shaughnessy," she said. "Brigid O'Shaughnessy. Yours?"

I told her.

"Need a ride somewhere?"

"Sure. I want to go see a cop named Dundy."

"Finish your eggs and I'll take you."

"Thanks," I said.

"Don't mention it."

Breakfast was setting up shop nice and warm inside me by the time we got to the downtown station. Dundy was his ever gracious self. "What the Sam Hill do you want?"

"Top of the morning to you, too," I said. "I want my manuscript."

"We haven't located it yet. And, frankly, I'm not all that interested in playing bloodhound for the likes of you."

"Well maybe you'd be interested to know I was snatched the minute I walked out of here by a gun-toting jay bird who took me to a car driven by Joel Nairobi."

"Nairobi? That little Arabian guy who smells like flowers?"

"Moroccan more likely, and the flowers are gardenia. Then maybe you'd be interested that the two of them escorted me to a nicely appointed hotel room fully occupied by one Hillary Horton Malloy."

"And just who is Hillary Horton Malloy?"

"A powerful atheist, sometimes known as 'the fat lady.' "

"How fat is she?"

"She could make a hula hoop cry."

Dundy gently rubbed his stomach. "Being fat ain't a crime in this state. Yet."

"But being slipped a *mickey* is."

"You were drugged?"

"When I sipped her complimentary 7-Up, I took a nose-dive into slumberland and woke up in some house out in Palmdale, guarded by a couple of goons. Now are you interested?"

Dundy looked at me, then at the girl. "Who's this?" he said.

"Miss Brigid O'Shaughnessy, the actress. She's a friend of mine."

Sniveling, Dundy said, "Don't ever make friends with a lawyer."

"Thanks a lot, Dundy," I said. "Now tell me about the manuscript. Who was the last one to see it?"

"Archie Miles."

"And who is Archie Miles?"

"The evidence booking officer."

"Can I talk to him?"

Dundy smiled, not a good sign. "You're welcome to try," he said coyly.

"Where is he?"

"The city morgue."

Brigid gave a little wheeze of surprise. My own skin began to gather up in little goose bumps. I said, "Don't these dead bodies set off a little signal?"

"What sort of signal?"

"Like an alarm. Like whenever this manuscript turns up, somebody dies. Or gets drugged. Or followed. Or lied to. There's something big going down, something involving atheism, evolution, money, and even possibly Geraldo Rivera."

Simultaneously, Brigid and Dundy said, *"Geraldo Rivera!"*

"That's what I said."

"Boy," Dundy muttered. "This really *is* big."

"What do we do next?" said Brigid.

I said, "Ever been to the city morgue?"

XXXIII

Grace indeed is a funny thing, I thought, for I had been graced with Darwin's death. With the old man out of the way, with no more threat that he would repudiate his own theories, I could easily pursue the next phase of my plot: the infiltration of evolutionary ideas into different spheres of influence. In this way would a new religion take hold, a secular religion, replacing the old traditions rooted in my ancient enemy, the God of Abraham, Isaac, Jacob, and Jesus.

Darwin would never have allowed some of the wild connections I was able to establish. But he was dead, so I made them.

My first move was to take Spencer's attractive phrase "survival of the fittest" and start throwing it around as a summary statement for evolution. It had such a nice ring to it, suggesting as it did that the fittest (the best, the cream of the crop) would survive (rise to the top, beat out the weaklings). This notion was close to any Englishman's heart, and I also knew it would play well with those ruffians over the sea, my next object, the Americans.

America! Land of the free and home of the gullible!

America! Where every man was a king and potentially a god!

America, where sweatshops abounded in dirty tenements while children were forced to manufacture things like cigars!

America, where people were nuttier for a game of football between Princeton and Yale than for religion!

America, where they shot their presidents![22]

Yes, the death of God would come most forcefully and thoroughly by way of America!

XXXIV

Things happened in America.

For instance: I was on the train from New York to Chicago once and was repulsed by the sight of a mother and daughter. The little girl couldn't have been more than seven years old. She was following her youthful instincts by pulling at the hat on a gentleman seated behind her. The gentleman smiled good-naturedly the first time but not the second. Finally, the mother intervened and said, "Dear, you mustn't bother the nice man."

"Why not?" the little girl asked.

"Because it is not polite. The man perhaps does not want to be bothered."

"So?" replied the little girl, and my heart immediately went out to her. Such questioning of authority! This little girl would make a great atheist some day! But then the mother said, "Other people's feelings are important to God. And God sees everything we do."

Cursed mother! I thought. *Cursed propagandist!* How long would we have to endure this tommyrot? How long would we allow parents to indoctrinate their young?

And then I had a thought. Why shouldn't children have the right to resist this sort of brainwashing? Why couldn't there be some sort of arm of the state entrusted to oversee the rearing of children? Why couldn't that agency have the power to remove children from the home when the parents stepped over the line from feeding and housing to educating in harmful doctrines?

My mind raced to form the steps. We would have to first consign religion to a substandard place on our hierarchy of values. Then we would have to ban it altogether from the schools. Then we would have to declare it actually harmful, like ancient superstitions. From that point, it would be easy.

It was a lovely daydream. But I knew that's all it was.[23]

I noticed the little girl looking at me. I smiled at her and she smiled back. She had striking eyes. Something passed between us; it was as if we understood each other completely.

I heard the woman call her daughter "Margaret." How was I to know that I would one day associate with that very girl when she was all grown up, that she would remember my face and would join me in a most important venture?

The gentleman she was bothering came down the aisle and asked if he could sit across from me. He had a rather craggy face, a large forehead and intelligent, skeptical eyes. My kind of man. We began talking.

"What is your line of work, sir?" I asked.

"This is it," he said, indicating the car in which we sat. "I am legal counsel for the railroad."

We made small talk for awhile, until he gradually revealed that he was interested in more things than just the law. He had a breadth of learning that was fascinating, and he was especially interested in human nature. That is what proved to be our meeting point.

"I am particularly interested in the criminal," he commented. "Why do men do the heinous things they do? Free will? Or, more likely, are these things inevitable, the product of causes that have come before?"

I perked up. "Are you saying that man has no free will?"

"And why should that be so surprising? Hasn't Darwin taught us that we are basically machines?"

"Why yes, Darwin has taught us something like that."

"And what will does a machine have? No, we are the product of forces beyond our control. We are biological mechanisms. We ought to institute social policy on this basis, not on outmoded concepts such as man's free will. This is all residual superstition from the Bible. Do you agree?"

"Me? Ah, yes. Yes I do agree. But it is still quite controversial to talk of these things, is it not?"

"It must be done. The truth shall set us free, to coin a phrase."

I extended my hand. "You, sir, are a man whose acquaintance I definitely wish to make. My name is Sir Max Busby."

"Clarence Darrow," he answered.

Ah, what a train ride that was! Clarence Darrow, who would one day deliver for me the greatest public relations blow to religion that was ever dealt. And the little girl I would later come to know as the woman Margaret Sanger![24]

Yes, America was fertile soil indeed.

XXXV

I found my best and most willing dupes in the universities. This never ceased to amaze me. If ever there was a last bastion of resistance against the unproved assumptions of Darwinism, it should have been In the seats of higher learning. Here was where the flaws in logic and holes in the evidence should have been held up in the classroom for all to see. But it wasn't so. The university professor was a quick recruit, driven by some inner need to latch onto a new idea. Whatever for? Why so sudden a conversion? I thought long and hard about it and finally decided the answer was simple.

The truth was dull, but evolution was exciting and gave them something daring to talk about. The one great fear of the university professor is that he shall be found boring—to his colleagues, to his students, and to himself. Boredom is a fate worse than falsity for this breed.

So it became a simple matter of dangling the prospect of new, evolutionary truths in front of these professors, not just in the realm of pure science, but in other fields as well.

Once they got the picture, they ran around like clucking chickens in search of golden eggs.

Some of the best chickens were found at Yale.

William Graham Sumner was a young economist and philosopher who taught at Yale, an institution that was at one time dedicated to training men for the proclaiming of the gospel. Now, of course, it taught evolution. I delighted in the irony.

What Sumner proved to be was a "missing link" between Darwinism and all out economic anarchy, which would exploit the poor, justify illegal trade practices, and generally create an atmosphere of rampant beastliness.

I had begun to see the wonderful effects of pure, economic Darwinism on people. For the rich, it was a pleasant justification for their station in life, and thus did away with the concept that God was behind their good fortune, and that they might owe part of it to Him. For the poor, it was a vehicle for their exploitation, especially children, and would very possibly crush their spirits as well as their bodies.

Once again, of course, a segment of the church was opposed to my plans, speaking out against the treatment of the lower classes. They quoted Jesus Christ quite a lot.

To Sumner, I quoted greed.

"What does a Yale professor make these days?" I asked him pointedly.

"A few hundred and benefits," he said.

"Not exactly the stuff of the fittest, eh?"

He nodded. I then offered to provide a yearly stipend to finance his research into the philosophical question, "How may Darwinism be a positive influence on the economic system of the United States?"

I suggested, "Wouldn't it be exciting to discover that millionaires are the naturally selected agents of society for certain work? Then, their lives of luxury could be justified on the ground that the bargain is a good one for society. The perceived negatives would only be seen as a minor cost of raising the social status."

"Hmmm." Sumner's eyes widened as if to take in new vistas.

A year later, he published the first of many articles arguing that very point.

[Editor's Note: Sir Max did not live to see Darwinian religion established in the universities, as it is today. So established is it that heretics are burned at the scholastic stake. In late 1993, a biology professor at San Francisco State University, Dean Kenyon, was ordered silenced for pointing out flaws in the Darwinian view and evidence for intelligent design. Kenyon, a world-class scientist and recognized expert on chemical evolutionary theory, had come to the conclusion that the Darwinian model was baseless. When Kenyon challenged the threat to his academic freedom, he was yanked from teaching biology classes and reassigned to innocuous lab work.

XXXVI

Again, a memory floats of its own accord across the landscape of my ancient brain.

It is Vienna, around 1907. I am walking the streets, taking in the sights, when I stop in a Tobbo shop for a coffee. As I sip, I sense I am being watched by a skinny young man with darting eyes sitting alone at a table in the corner. He appears to be sketching something.

I motion for this obviously destitute lad to join me. I buy him a coffee in exchange for a look at his sketch.

It is awful. It is supposed to be me, but it looks like a tree-dwelling sloth in a cape.

I tell the young man as much, and his head bows. He tells me he was just denied admission to the Academy of Fine Arts. He feels his life is at an end.

Perfect.

For where such a sorrowful life exists, it may be turned to other purposes. I pause a moment to let my imagination run. I ask what he thinks of Darwinism as it relates to his station in life.

"What do you mean, sir?" he asks.

"Why, it is obvious. According to the principal of survival of the fittest, you are about to be snuffed out by forces stronger than yourself. If I were a young buck like you, with no talent for drawing, I should spend my days discovering which forces were seeking my demise, and resolve to use all my strengths and abilities to fight back, and perhaps destroy such forces."

As usually happened with my chance encounters, an illumination explodes in the young man's head.

"I wonder what forces those might be?" he ponders.

And then, almost as a throwaway, I say, "The Jews."

That's when it happens. The illumination inside him leaps into his eyes. Like a man possessed, he suddenly stands upon his chair and begins regaling the habitués of the Tobbo shop with a fiery speech about world domination by the Semites.

The owner swiftly acts, grabs the young man by the collar and throws him out the door. As he comes back he looks at me and says, "I am tired of that freeloader Hitler! He is allowed in my shop no more!"

"Hitler?"

"Adolf Hitler, a malingerer."

As quickly as my ninety-eight-year-old body can go, I am outside the shop, calling to the back of the young man. "Herr Hitler! The man who owns this shop, his real name is Goldstein!"

I have heard lately that this once destitute and failed art student is now something of a wheel in German politics. I wonder if he will do any damage.[25]

XXXVII

I next turned my attentions to Harvard University. Again, I found it ironic that an institution founded to train ministers was now so willing to change into one that would lay the foundation for the death of faith in God.

Harvard had a law school where the professors taught what law schools had been teaching for hundreds of years, that "the law" was something which existed outside of nature—it was handed down by a Supreme Being. This was the legacy of Sir William Blackstone.

Blackstone, author of the famous *Commentaries* (1769), enunciated a jurisprudence where the role of the judge was to *find* the law, through application of logic and deduction. This gave rise to a well ordered system of precedent and *stare decisis*.

I, of course, didn't like this system, for it presupposed a Law Giver.

But what if evolutionary theory were placed on top of the law? What if we saw laws as struggling for survival, like animals in the wild? What would be the result?

The result would be human beings making laws as they went along and trying to justify them *post hoc*. It would rule out the need for a divine being!

Then laws would arise from the prevailing societal mood. When enough citizens and enough judges felt that the world should be ordered a certain way (not paying any attention to the order set down by divine decree) they could then claim that this certain way had "value."

How could it have value? Simply because it would be seen as a "social good" by the opinion makers.

Ah, how I delighted in my own, wicked cogitations!

Suppose, one day, enough of the intelligentsia got together and decided it would be a good thing to (oh, let's take a wild example) allow women to terminate their pregnancies before birth. Such a thing would be inconceivable under revealed law. Revealed law, primarily the Bible, mandated that life began at conception, that the unborn child had rights like the rest of the human family, and so forth. In effect, under that scheme of things God gave a law, and a fundamental right to life.

But under my plan, that would no longer be a hindrance. Eventually, judges could look at society and say, "Well, it appears as though enough women want this opportunity that we should give it whack. We can define life as beginning at some point after conception, draw some sort of arbitrary line, and have at it."

And the right to abortion could then be deemed "fundamental" to society. We could turn revealed law on its head!

I was dizzy with the prospect, though I knew America would probably never sink so low as to allow abortion on demand.

So, I went to see the dean of the law school,

Christopher Langdell. He was fascinated with my idea. And the engine of evolution chugged forward.

Harvard changed its theory of law to the evolutionary model, and things have never been the same there since.[26]

That was the whole point, of course. Evolution, when carried to its natural conclusion, absolutely did away with objective morality. If we are only chance beings, we answer to no one but chance and ourselves. The strongest selves will rule. No one can propose any moral claim which is universally binding!

And God would be out of the scene completely.

A few people recognized this, of course, and attempted to point it out. Disraeli, for one, was particularly galling to me, because his pen was so sharp. One of his fictional characters said, "Instead of Adam, our ancestry is traced to the most grotesque of creatures, thought is phosphorous, the soul complex nerves, and our moral sense a secretion of sugar."

Oh, ho, I thought. That's rich. A secretion of sugar. He was right, of course, but I did not like being made sport of.

That's also why I didn't like the wag who came up with this:

Darwin set forth,

In a book of much worth,

The importance of Nature's selection;

How the struggle for life

Is a laudable strife,

And results in specific distinction.

Let pigeons and doves

Select their own loves,

And grant them a million of ages,

Then doubtless you'll find

They've altered their kind,

And turned into prophets and sages.[27]

Very funny, I thought. But you see what was happening? A cultural backlash! Whenever an idea becomes the object of ridicule in the public discourse, you are in trouble. You have to take immediate action.

It was time for another forgery.

Only this time, it had to be big. It had to be a link. Yes, it had to be an early man. That was all I would settle for.

But I was not up to the task alone. I had to recruit someone to help me. It had to be a special someone, someone without morals or ethics, who would not hesitate to stoop to whatever means necessary in order to baldly deceive as many people as possible.

In other words, I needed a lawyer.

Fortunately for me, the perfect specimen was close at hand.

XXXVIII

Charles Dawson was a lawyer in Sussex and something of a fossil collector. He had, in fact, presented a collection of fossilized reptile bones to the British Museum in 1887. I knew the "bone keeper" there quite well, one Arthur Smith-Woodward, and he had told me a little about this Dawson fellow.

He was rather a snob, this Dawson, and wanted nothing more than to be the one to find the "missing link." His desire was intensified with the discovery of Heidelberg Man, a jaw with modern looking teeth[28] found in the Gunz-Mindel interglacial deposits in Germany. To think of finding out that the original man was a Kraut! No snobbish Englishman of the day could stand such a horrible thought. Smith-Woodward told me Dawson was beside himself with anxiety.

Thus, when I scheduled my appointment with Dawson in January of 1908, I expected to find a willing conspirator. I was not disappointed.

But first, we had to dance about a bit.

"Smithy tells me you were aboard the *Beagle*," Dawson said, puffing a pipe.

"Quite right. I can say I was connected with the modern theory of evolution from before its beginning."

"How I envy you, sir."

"Yes, but these are dark days for the theory, I'm afraid. And what with the Germans unearthing early man—" I let that sink in. "Does the name Piltdown mean anything to you?"

He thought about it a moment. "It's a gravel pit, isn't it? Somewhere around Haywards Heath?"

"That's right. That's exactly right."

"Well, what of it?"

"I was just thinking, what an apt place to find some bones, if you know what I mean? What better place than an English gravel pit to unearth some evidence of our ancestry?"

His eyes twinkled slightly at the prospect. "Ah, if only it were so. But what are the chances? Is there something about Piltdown you know?"

I sat back, playing my fish a little, giving him some slack. "I have an instinct for these sorts of things. Did you know I actually showed Darwin where to find his first iguana?"

"You don't say?"

"But I do say. Now, you do grant that finding the missing link would be of monumental importance, do you not?"

"Oh, I grant, I grant."

"And that the man who makes such a find shall become famous, forever in the books as the one to connect Darwin's theory to the human being."

I could see he was practically dizzy with the prospect. The pipe had lapsed, and Dawson made no attempt to reignite it. His mind was spinning behind his brown eyes, as if he were formulating some grand speech to make in front of a jury, or maybe he was envisioning his bust, placed alongside Darwin's in the British Museum.

I let him remain in his trance a few moments, then said, "Such immortality, why, it would almost be worth doctoring a little of the evidence, eh?"

That brought him back to earth. "Doctoring? Evidence?"

"Come, come, barrister, you mean to say you never tip-tapped any evidence in your own cases before?" I put on a coy little smile, and winked.

He smiled. "Sir Max, you are a man after my own heart."

Yes, I thought, *what there is of it.*

XXXIX

By a stroke of fortune, we managed to drag the Church into our scheme, by way of a renegade priest with a thing for rocks.

Teilhard de Chardin was an odd duck. A Jesuit pale-ontologist! What would they think of next?[29]

But I liked him because he had this idea rolling around in his head like loose limestone—that evolution was true, but proceeded along some line compelled by the universe. That was delicious. An evolutionist priest fleeing the Church! A mystical evolutionist no scientist would say "boo" to! In short, a wacky sort of fellow who would become a third "witness" to our "find."

He eagerly joined the plot and we planned it thus.

Dawson would go digging around in Piltdown imme-diately and find some thick, fossilized skull fragments. That would do it. Then we would wait three years. No sense in making this all look *too* good.

In 1911, he would find more fragments that matched the first. At that time, he'd notify Smith-Woodward and the British Museum, and take representatives along on future digs. Teilhard would join in then, to give the effect of just coming on board.

Then, with Smith-Woodward watching and Teilhard

out someplace else, Dawson would make the first of our double barreled finds—an ape-like jawbone.

It would be broken at the hinges and on the point, so as to be difficult to place along with the skull fragments we'd planted and dug up earlier.

And, of course, one vital clue would be missing, the clue that would establish whether or not this jaw belonged to a primate or an early man—the canine teeth.

It worked to perfection.

XL

In December 1912, before the London Geological Society, the discovery of "Dawson's Dawn Man" was announced.

The first man was British! The empire was redeemed! Dawson and Teilhard became instantly famous.

I was content to stay behind the scenes, getting ready to put the capper (you'll pardon the joke, which will become apparent) on the whole adventure. It occurred on the night of August 29, 1913.

Dawson, Teilhard, and I huddled together in Dawson's flat. "Did you bring it?" I asked the Jesuit.

Teilhard pulled a small, cloth sack from his pocket and dangled it before us.

"Well, come on, let's see it," Dawson insisted.

Teilhard pulled the sack open, shook it over the table and the thing fell out.

We all just looked at it for a moment.

"Magnificent," said Dawson.

"Superb," I said.

"Cosmic," said Teilhard.

It was one of the missing canine teeth, the final proof that Dawson's Man was indeed a man and not a beast.

Of course it was a phony—filed, colored, and packed with grains of sand.

"When will Smith-Woodward get here?" I asked.

"Seven o'clock tomorrow morning," said Dawson.

"Good." I turned to Teilhard. "What are you waiting for, a sign?"

He understood. He left immediately to plant the tooth in the fossil rich soil of Piltdown.

They excavated a trench—Teilhard, Dawson, Smith-Woodward and some others. Teilhard found the tooth.

The world now knows of it as Piltdown Man. With the help of the British Museum, this fraud was never discovered.

I wonder if the truth will ever be known.[30]

XLI

Ah, here it is again, a shadowy memory peering out from behind my cerebral cortex.

This time, I see a skinny bloke with a pipe, doodling numbers on a napkin in the commons of Trinity College, Cambridge. It is somewhere around 1912, and I ask the odd numbersmith what on earth he is doing.

He looks up at me and with a perfectly straight face says, "I am constructing a mathematics system based upon purely logical notions and concepts."

"Terrific," I say. I do not know what this man is talking about, but I sense about him an intellectual vigor that can prove useful if turned in the right direction. "Would you like to take a break?"

He heaves a sigh and puts down his pencil. I introduce myself and ask him what he thinks of the work of Charles Darwin.

"Life changing," he says. "In a way, it provided my salvation. I was raised by a puritan grandmother, you know."

"No, I don't know, I just met you."

He seems not to hear. "Darwin showed me that her kind of God was unnecessary. Oh, if only I were not a philosopher who has to save the world through certainty! I would most definitely save the world by ridding it of its vile superstitions."

I pounce. "Good sir, forget your numerology. You have a great work of service to do mankind by writing of the obsolescence of God!"

For a moment, his eyes glisten. "But there is no money in it," he says, making a perfectly pragmatic and irrefutable point. But I do not give up. When one is 113 years old, one gets set in one's ways.

"Some day," I say, "I think you could write a book that would generate enough controversy to bring you a pretty penny. Why, such a book might be called *Reasons for Not Being a Christian* or some such. Just think of it! You would be first in line and might cause the floodgates to open!"

Again, I see a dancing in his deep-set orbs.

But just as quickly it is gone. "I *must* prove that one plus one equals two, with absolute logic. It is not easy!" He waves me off and picks up his pencil once more.

So I have had no luck with this most interesting chap. He might have been a great one for my plans.

As I stand to leave, I notice his name scrawled across a notebook on the table. The name is Bertrand Russell.[31]

The city morgue had a medicine smell you could've ridden a skateboard on. The lady at reception, who might have been the model for the mother's corpse in *Psycho,* made me fill out the usual forms. We were ushered into "central," where the ice boxes are.

A deputy M.E. pulled out a drawer marked "Miles, Archie." Brigid gasped at her first up-close look at a dead body. "Easy," I said. Then to the M.E.: "Cause of death?"

"Suicide," he said.

"By what means?"

"Necktie party for one."

"Hanged himself?"

The M.E. nodded.

"That the coroner's official position?" I asked.

"What of it?"

"Nothing. Where was he found?"

"In his apartment."

"Uh-huh. Well, thanks. You've been a great help."

The M.E. thrust Miles' drawer back into the box.

I took Brigid over to Pink's and let her buy me a hot dog. "So we're at a dead end?" she said, attacking her Coney Island. She paused, smiled, and said, "You'll pardon the expression?"

"Not really."

"What do you mean?"

"I mean somebody bought off the coroner. That suicide rap is bogus."

Brigid blinked. "How do you know?"

"Listen," I said, "in a hanging you get an inverted 'V' bruise on the neck, because the body hangs down and the rope hangs up. Miles' bruise was a straight line. Another thing: unless you get a judicial hanging from a gallows, the bruise isn't stark. Most suicides by hanging end up as suffocation, not a broken neck. Miles supposedly killed himself in his apartment. That would mean kicking away a chair at most. You wouldn't get a deep bruise like Miles had from that."

Eyes wide, Brigid said, "How do you know all that?"

"I worked on a few murder cases when I was with the DA's office. You pick this stuff up."

"So what are you saying?"

"I'm saying Miles was murdered. There was a small bruise at the base of Miles' neck. That's where the hitman's hand was pressing as the rope or silk tightened. This always uses more pressure than necessary, which accounts for the deepness of the neck contusion. You also get obstructed blood vessels so the face and neck become deep, dark red, consistent with Miles' blotched appearance."

"Wow," said Brigid. "So who would want to kill him?"

"I'm not sure," I said. I took a paper napkin and laid it out on the table. With a pen I made four dots, and marked them respectively—Malloy, Coroner, Geraldo Rivera, Miles. I made a question mark and wrote "Dundy?" next to it. "All we have to do is connect the dots."

"Where shall we start?" said Brigid, excitedly.

"Ever been a guest on a talk show?"

XLII

I noted these developments during the first part of the new century:

1. Evolution became more and more an accepted fact among the clergy. Many ministers jumped on the progressive bandwagon, seeking not to be thought intellectual buffoons for refusing to absorb evolutionary thinking. It was easy for these to mythologize away the book of Genesis. All very much according to plan.

2. I continued to receive praise and remuneration from scientific associations.

3. The pizza pie was invented in 1905, in New York City.

4. In 1906, a murderer attempted to justify his crime by citing social Darwinism. Survival of the fittest, he said, meant that he could kill those less fit than himself. In this case, his father-in-law was the subnormal specimen. The argument, much as I liked it, did not find a sympathetic ear with the judiciary, and the man was hanged. I had faith that the court system, once Darwinism thoroughly took over,[32] would one day allow this defense.

5. In 1907, I visited a sweatshop, and watched people being treated like cattle. Exploited by the more advanced of our kind. Fine, fine, fine.

6. The Model T Ford came out in 1908 and sold for $850. I hired a driver and was able to get around quite

handily. I enjoyed honking the horn and scaring animals and small children.

7. In 1909, I arranged for an American tour led by Dr. Sigmund Freud, one of my greatest creations. Freud was an atheist and a dreamer. He had devised a system of explanations for the human condition that had nothing to do with man's supposed "nature," but rather his upbringing. This was tremendous! No longer would it be necessary to talk about an inherent nature, but of early sexual trauma! Under my prompting (and my endless supply of Cuban cigars) Siggy also went further, and said God was simply a wishful projection borne of our insecurities. A great asset, Dr. Freud.

8. In 1910, Jack Johnson, a Negro, defeated Jim Jeffries, a white man, in a heavyweight championship boxing match. As a result, race riots broke out in various parts of the country, and several Negroes were killed by whites. This proved to me evolutionary thinking was infusing the masses. Why shouldn't the white race consider itself a "higher form" of life, and try by force to destroy its competitors? Under Darwinism, such thinking not only couldn't be denied, it was inevitable.

XLIII

Then there arose a "thorn in my flesh," as it were. It was something called "Fundamentalism," a term and phenomenon that would haunt me for years.

I had taken up residence in New York City, the cultural capital of America, intent on playing the role of grease to the inexorable machinery of evolutionary thought.

In that role I gave speeches from time to time, always to a friendly audience. Preaching to the choir, as it were. Americans seem to have a fixation on celebrity. If you can establish yourself as one, there is no end to the respect and monetary rewards you can milk out of the Yanks.

The Society of Scientists, New York Branch, held monthly meetings in the smoking room at the Algonquin Hotel. These were self-congratulatory affairs, an excuse to give and receive pats on the back for experimental hijinks and hypothetical speculations. Naturally, all were now Darwinists, for not to be one was socially unacceptable. (That is really the history of evolution in a nutshell.)[33]

The dull brown and dim lighting at the Algonquin seemed to me at the time a marked contrast to what we were about—enlightenment! Light to the world! What were we doing here in this dark cavern of an inn? No matter. I was the honored guest.

The evening wore on with the usual long-winded

speeches and presentations, and then I was introduced by the president of the group, Dr. Phillip Phatt.

Enthusiastic applause brought me to the lectern. "Mr. President, members of the Society. I thank you for that warm introduction. But I can't help thinking, it wasn't nearly as warm as those dreadful Galapagos Islands!"

They laughed, as audiences always did, at my inside joke. It was not socially acceptable to refrain from laughing at any inside joke. I continued, "Those were heady days, my friends. We were not at all certain our theory would be given a hearing, let alone respect. Quite the contrary, we had many enemies back then, I can tell you!"

I paused for a sip of water. And that is when it happened.

A voice from the back of the room shouted, "Fraud!"

A chorus of "harrumphs" arose from the assemblage, and heads turned. I squinted, but alas my failing orbs (survival of the fittest indeed!) could not bring into focus the shape standing in the rear shadows.

"Fraud!" the voice repeated, a clear manful voice, full of vigor. "Why don't you tell the truth? Evolution is a lie!"

Dr. Phatt had risen from the head table and faced the back (he did not move toward it, probably for fear this was an anarchist or madman). "See here," Phatt said. "What is the meaning of this?"

The form moved slowly forward, into what little light there was. He was a nicely groomed young man, probably thirty years old. "The meaning of this is fraud! Evolution is a fraud and everyone knows it! You are all part of a conspiracy!"

"By what right do you come in here and accuse us of such things?" Phatt said.

"By right of the First Amendment to the Constitution of the United States of America!"

"The—the what?" Phatt stammered.[34]

"Free speech. The exchange of ideas. Only you're perpetrating a fraud that will send souls into hell!"

So that was it. Some sort of religious fanatic. I stepped in. "We do not need your hysteria here, young man. Please remove yourself."

"Hysteria? Then how about a real debate, on the merits? What has science produced, what one thing, to prove this theory? You think questions like this are hysterical? Just wait until the people catch on to what you're really up to, and you'll see a wave of revolt that will make hysteria seem tame!"

What nonsense was he spouting?

"We are Christians who have not abandoned the faith. We hold to the fundamentals of God's revelation, and nothing more or less. And we have declared war on you, the enemies of the truth, and we will not rest until we take captive every evil thought!"

Unnoticed during this exchange was Dr. Phatt, who had slipped out to alert hotel security, which at the

Algonquin in those days was a 250-pound Irishman, one O'Kelly, who could usually be found at the bar. He gladly slipped in now for a little action.

"Come on now, me boy," said O'Kelly as he approached the youth. "Let's take a little walk." The young man did not protest, nor did he speak again. But on the way out he looked at me, pouring his eyes into mine. They were not so much eyes of anger, as his rhetoric would have suggested. They were, instead, something much more insulting. Eyes of pity! As if I needed his pity! As if he knew I was, yes, on my way to hell! That was the disturbing part.

So disturbing, in fact, that I could not continue my remarks. Phatt and the others understood and spent the rest of the evening apologizing profusely. They told me just to forget the whole thing.

But I could not forget it. "They," whoever they were, had declared war. Who were "they?" Where were they located? What was this all about? Was there really a threat? If so, I would have to deal with it. Anything was possible in America!

So I made an appointment with the leading clergyman in the city, Reverend Melville Cackle of the Fifth Avenue Collegiate Church who proved to be an enormous help.

XLIV

How influential was Reverend Melville Cackle?

Let's put it this way. In his church worshiped the mayor of New York and half the City Council. Three United States presidents, when they were in town, had gone to Fifth Avenue Collegiate to hear the famed orator. He was quoted in at least one speech by President McKinley (who referred to him as "that pillar of righteousness").

A striking fifty-year-old, well coifed and mannered, Reverend Cackle filled his three-piece suit to the bursting point. The ample girth belied an indulgent lifestyle, as perhaps befitted the leading preacher in New York City. Cackle entertained me in his study, a comfortably furnished room overlooking New York's most traveled street.

"It is an honor," Reverend Cackle began, "to have you here, Sir Max. An honor indeed. I have read about your colorful life."

"You have?" There was no reason for him to know anything about me.

"Oh, yes." He reached for a pipe, filled the bowl with tobacco. "I have many interests outside the day to day of the church." In true, orator style he paused to let this fact sink in, taking the time to light his pipe. I smelled the tobacco. It was rich. The man apparently spared no expense on his vice.

"You see, Sir Max, the world of today is one of flux, of change. The modern man, if he is to keep up, must spend his time in study and contemplation of the currents of the age. One of these is, of course, the evolutionary theory. And you have played no small part in that story, am I right?"

"Right you are."

"Right. Now, tell me, what may I do for you?" Cackle placed one hand on his enormous width and smiled even as his teeth clenched his pipe.

"I have a religious question, and I am told you are the man with the answers."

Puff puff. "As I said, I must keep up. I try to have answers for the man on the street as well as for progressive men such as yourself." I liked that word, "progressive."

I recounted my speech and the heckler's interruption, and repeated what he had said. Cackle nodded, with a look of complete understanding. "Ah," he said. "A Fundamentalist."

"A Fundawhat?"

"Fundamentalist. A regrettable sect that has sprung up within the church."

"That's what they call themselves? The Fundamentalist Sect?"

He laughed, amused at my confusion. "No, no. They don't call themselves that. We do. They would have us believe they are merely Christians, the true Christians, the ones loyal to the ancient faith, if you can believe that nonsense."[35]

"Excuse me, did you say 'nonsense'?"

"I did so, advisedly."

Now this was curious. "So these people, these Fundamentalists, they are in reality enemies of the Church?"

A thick cloud of pipe smoke wafted my way. I worried for an instant about my decomposing respiratory system. Cackle said, "I don't think they will ever amount to a real threat to progress. They have a few vocalists who keep carping on the inerrancy of the Bible."

"Inerrancy?"

"Yes, they really hang their hat on that one. Imagine, with all we know about the Bible today! The Bible is a flawed, ancient book, just like other flawed ancient books. The Krauts have taught us that!"[36]

"But you preach from the Bible, don't you?"

"Yes, but I can pick and choose. If something in it supports my point, I use it, as I might use Shakespeare or Mark Twain."

"You put the Bible in the same category as Shakespeare or Mark Twain?"

"There is no functional difference."

Wonderful! I couldn't have asked for anything better from the spiritual leader of New York City! And what wonderfully pompous language—"no *functional* difference." It was the sort of language an intellectual would use when trying to justify an absurd premise. What is more absurd than denigrating the authority of the Book from which you get your authority? This is what the "liberal theologians" were doing with their self-contradictory project to tear down the Bible. How I longed for more Cackles! Enough of them and Christianity would self-destruct.

These Fundamentalists, though, troubled me.

"What do you think we can do about this Fundamentalist problem?" I said.

"I've given it much thought. I should probably say more about it from the pulpit. I need to educate my people. Many of them still have old ideas about the Bible. If I warn them of the perils of Fundamentalism, they'll listen."

I left after having secured an agreement from Cackle to preach vigorously against this dreaded, upstart movement. That, I assumed, would be the end of Fundamentalism's threat.

Was I ever wrong.

XLV

Cackle was as good as his word. The Sunday following our meeting he delivered a fiery sermon, enflamed so as to gain significant space in the *New York Times*.

[Editor's Note: The following news clipping was glued to the pages of Busby's manuscript]

REVEREND CACKLE WARNS OF EVILS OF FUNDAMENTALISM

In an eloquent plea for progress, the Reverend Melville Cackle, senior pastor at the Fifth Avenue Collegiate Church, warned his flock of the movement known as "Fundamentalism," emphasizing to the congregation that "we must move forward from the shadows of our superstitious past."

Speaking for an hour to a packed auditorium, Reverend Cackle began by outlining the features of this movement. "They are really fanatics who are afraid of the truth," said Cackle, citing their aversion to Darwin's theory of evolution as one example. "Evolution is as true as the nose on your face," Reverend Cackle said to the appreciative gathering. "And that same nose can help you smell the stench that Fundamentalism is spreading."

Cackle delivered eight more messages that year on the same theme. Then one night he ate an undercooked chicken and dropped dead.

XLVI

Fundamentalism had lost a hardy foe. I thought perhaps Cackle's influence would reach beyond his death and soon Fundamentalism would fade. I was unprepared for its vigor, as the following account will attest.

I was walking through Chelsea one afternoon when I found myself face to face with the young zealot who had interrupted my speech before the Society of Scientists.

"Good day," he said jovially.

"You have the temerity to wish me good day?" I said, recognizing him at once.

"Of course. I have no personal quarrel with you, only with your views. It is your ideas that are dangerous."

"By what right do you question scientific truth?"

From under his arm he pulled out what appeared to be a well read Bible. "This is the truth. And by its light we can see the fraudulent nature of all untruth."

"Your Bible, sir, is the fraud!" I shouted.

"What makes you say that?" he answered calmly.

"The facts, sir, the facts! Evolution has shown that we have evolved from lower forms of life. Therefore, your sacred book is wrong."

"Can you give me a single 'fact' which shows that we have evolved from lower forms of life?"

Quickly, I said, "Piltdown Man."

The young preacher smiled. "I have no doubt that this is a fabrication."

I shuddered slightly but recovered. "Beyond that, one can simply look at nature and see that it lacks a designer."

"Untrue," the preacher said. "One can see in nature the very hand of God. It is the lenses of the observer that matter most."

"Lenses?"

"Yes. Looking through the lens of faith, confident in the reliability of God, I can see His work. On the other hand, those who wish only to believe in blind nature can see only blindness and chance at work."

"I do not 'believe' in nature, sir. Nature is what *is*. There is no faith involved."

"Oh, but there is. For nature is only that which we can observe. What about the unobservable? Can you say there is no supernatural?"

"I can say so, confidently."

"Can you prove it?"

Now I was beginning to get annoyed. "Why should I have to prove anything to you?" I retorted.

Then he said a curious thing. "I do not wish you to prove anything to me. I wish you to prove it to yourself."

Cursed clergyman! He had tricked me into a conversation in which he was seeking my own welfare.

And then he said the most noxious thing I had ever heard. "I shall pray for you."

I raised my cane above my head. "You shall not! I do not want your cursed prayers!"

The preacher looked directly into my eyes. "But God wants *you*," he said. "And God usually gets what he wants."

With that, the preacher left me, and I was shaken.

Shaken because of the confident faith of this man in his Book. Shaken because he did not back down from what I thought were inviolable intellectual truths. And shaken most of all because I feared his prayers might, in some way beyond my understanding, be answered.

Now I knew that my foes, the people of the Book, the Bible believers, would have to be dealt with. I would have to close off their influence upon the general culture. I would have to devise a way to make them look like idiots. In short, I would have to score a major public relations victory.

Fortunately, I soon found the man who would become my eager weapon against the Fundamentalists of America.

XLVII

A young journalist was writing prose I particularly liked. He had a pen as sharp as a razor and, I perceived, an antipathy toward organized religion.

We met clandestinely at a bar in Baltimore, where he was employed. He puffed cigars as we spoke.

"So you were a colleague of Darwin, and involved in the Piltdown discovery," he said. "Impressive, Pops."

"Pops? What is this 'Pops'?" I said.

"American slang for 'older gentleman.' I'm kind of an authority on language."

"I see."

"I'm also an authority on people. And I can see you have something on your mind. Why don't you spill it?"

"Spill?"

"Tell, tell."

I didn't like his manner, but I thought it might prove effective for the long term.

"I'm concerned about the intellectual future of this country," I said.

"Join the club."

"What club?"

"That means 'I agree with you.'" He puffed his cigar

and looked me over. I stared back and knew I wouldn't have trouble with him. I had been sizing people up for a hundred years and could tell almost from the start of a conversation where it would lead. The bluster of this American scoundrel told me he had some deep insecurities. He was the type of man who needed enemies to make his life worthwhile, enemies he could excoriate. This is what made him feel important.

I continued, "To put it bluntly, sir, I'm looking to subsidize an intellectual who shares my concerns."

At the mention of money his eyes got a little wider. He tapped the ash of his cigar on the floor.

"What would you ask for in return?" he said.

"Merely a certain amount of material written in a suggested direction."

"I can't be bought."

"No one is implying that." It was best to allow him to feel he would be left alone to be his own man. "What I am looking for is simply a champion of certain values, someone to fight the fight, as they say."

"And what fight is that?"

"The fight against religious intolerance and anti-intellectualism."

He smiled. "I'm with you there, Doc."

"Doc?"

"Generic reference for any male."

"Quite."

And so began my association with H. L. Mencken. He was more than happy to accept my terms, to write with sarcasm and contempt about the Fundamentalists and all they stood for. He wrote some effective pieces then, but his most destructive work would not come until later, until the watershed event in the summer of 1925.

I shall next recount the circumstances which led up to that most auspicious moment in the history I am recording.

XLVIII

The law in America had the possibility of becoming putty in the hands of the right people.

The idea that law "evolves," which I first suggested to Langdell of Harvard, had caught on among the leading scholars of the day. Blackstone was largely forgotten, and the idea that there was a natural order to things, and objective moral values, was replaced with individual digestion. In other words, judges basically decided cases the way they wanted to decide them, influenced by whatever forces happened to be on hand at the time.[37]

What if the law could be used to reshape the country in an atheistic mode? The idea excited me to no end.

Imagine a country where the public espousal of Christian ideas would be outlawed. With a clever handling of the First Amendment to the American Constitution, and a handful of nonreligious judges, why, such a thing might have a chance.

And what about controlling the curriculum in public schools? Getting all mention of God out of the classroom? Perhaps that was wishing too much, but I dreamed.

What I needed was an organization to assist me as I pursued these avenues, a legal arm to my scheme as it were. And it had to have a catchy name, one that would capture the imaginations of a freedom-loving people while, at the same time, seek to destroy their society.

I decided, if I ever were to form such an organization, I would call it something like the "American Civil Liberties Union."

XLIX

In 1917 I attended a lecture at a union hall in New York City. The speaker was a young man named Roger Baldwin.

Baldwin was the head of a group called the National Civil Liberties Bureau of the American Union Against Militarism. He was speaking out against the Great War and was in favor of draft dodging. The basic thrust of his message was that American society was manipulative of individuals, and there was no "greater good" which justified this war for freedom.

I had found the man to head my legal organization. He readily accepted.

We corresponded for a time, discussed philosophy and direction. He seemed at the time a little too Utopian for my tastes, but as an atheist was useful to me nonetheless. He was zealous for the same goal I was—getting God out of the country.

So, in 1920, we founded the American Civil Liberties Union, or ACLU for short. Now it was simply a matter of using this organization for our purposes. We vigorously shopped for inroads into the established order of things.

Then, in 1924, a wonderful opportunity was presented, around which all of my life's work would come into bold focus.

"I'm here to see Geraldo Rivera."

"Do you have an appointment?"

"Not exactly."

"I'm afraid Mr. Rivera is very busy. He sees no one without an appointment."

The receptionist was a tough-looking lady, one who was obviously used to the refuse of L.A. trying to get in to see her boss whenever he was filming in town.

"Tell him I have Brigid O'Shaughnessy with me."

The receptionist looked at Brigid with a jaundiced eye. "And who is she supposed to be?"

"What if I told you she was O. J. Simpson's first wife?"

"We get dozens of those."

"Or that her father is a Mafia kingpin..."

"Old story."

"...who sold secrets to the Russians..."

The receptionist yawned.

"...and was the man behind the assassination of John F. Kennedy!"

"Look, mister," the receptionist said. "You'll have to do better than that. I'm afraid I couldn't get Geraldo out of his makeup chair with that story."

Scratching my cheek, I said, "Okay. Just tell him the fat lady and I want that manuscript back."

That set the receptionist back on her classified ads. "Wait here," she said. She got up and was buzzed through a glass door. I sat down with Brigid and winked at her.

The receptionist came back. "Mr. Rivera will see you now," she said.

Geraldo Rivera was fit and trim, a little shorter than I expected. He wore natty suspenders and a loosened, fruit salad tie. "Come in, come in," he said, ushering us into an office strewn with Geraldo pictures and memorabilia. "Please have a seat. I'm anxious to hear what you have to say."

"You and I are apparently interested in the same thing," I said. "A certain manuscript. An old one."

Geraldo tapped a pencil on his desk. "I'm interested in many things," he said.

"Like ratings?"

"In this business, we're all interested in ratings."

"Some more than others."

"What's your point?"

"The point is this. Suppose you, Geraldo Rivera, were to uncover an old manuscript that happened to be cultural dynamite? Wouldn't that possibly garner a cover on *Time* magazine?"

Geraldo said, "It might at that."

"And you wouldn't really care how you got it, would you? You wouldn't ask too many questions."

"Out with it, Mr. Bell. I don't have time for sermons."

"Okay, here's the way I see it. Someone came to you with the story of the Busby manuscript. When you found out what it contained, you snapped at it. You wanted it, and didn't care how. But another party, a certain fat lady, got wind of it, too. And she wanted it for a very different reason."

"What reason is that?"

"To destroy it."

This caught him off guard. "Why would she want to do that?" he said.

"It's a long story, beginning with the religious war unleashed by Darwinism in 1859."

"What religious war? It's science, isn't it?"

"That's what they would like you to believe. But this manuscript documents the true motivation of Darwinist dogma. It is, and always has been, a religious war. That's why Darwinists are so jealous about their position in society. They are like a priesthood, and they have torches ready to burn those who challenge them."

Geraldo smiled. "How would you like to be a guest on my show, Mr. Bell?"

Brigid nudged me in the ribs. I smiled, "No thanks," I said. "Do you have the manuscript? And did you know someone was murdered to get it to you?"

His genuine look of shock convinced me he wasn't aware of the circumstances. "Follow me," he said.

We followed him down a long hallway, past a series of offices, to a stairway in the back. Down we went into a dimly lit underbelly. Geraldo took out a key and unlocked a heavy door. He flicked on a bare light bulb, illuminating a room full of steel shelves. These were stuffed with boxes, papers, and files. "Over here," Geraldo said.

Brigid and I walked to a small table, and there it sat. The Busby manuscript. I lifted the cover to check its authenticity. It was the real deal.

"That's it," I said.

Geraldo nodded. "What a story, huh?"

Brigid said, "Put your hands in the air and back up."

I turned around and looked into the business end of a Ruger .22 caliber handgun. Geraldo and I put our hands in the air.

L

The children are the future. If evolutionism would be the force, once and for all, that ruled the nations, that became the new religion of the enlightened man, it would have to be hammered into young minds as early as possible.

Already, the revolutionary government known as the Soviet Union was using Darwin in order to rid the nation of "the opiate of the people," namely religion.

The same thing could happen in America.

But old beliefs die hard, and I found a resistance among the educators I contacted to the proposition of teaching Darwin in the schools. One state, Tennessee, had even passed laws against teaching the theory in the classroom.

What a development! What if it started a trend?

There was one man who wanted to see that trend take off. His name was William Jennings Bryan. With his World's Fundamental Association, this thrice defeated presidential candidate was making noises about two thirds of the states having anti-evolution laws, and eventually getting that doctrine into the Constitution!

The law being at issue, I returned once again to the offices of the ACLU.[38]

"Well, ladies and gentlemen, what are we going to do?" I asked.

"I'm glad you asked that, Max," said Baldwin. "There is someone I'd like you to meet."

He produced a young man he identified as one George Rappelyea. He was an unkempt looking youth, with brown eyes and horn-rimmed glasses. Baldwin said, "This fellow hates Fundamentalists."

"Admirable," I said. "But what good will that do us?"

"Tell him, George," said Baldwin.

George said, "I think I can arrange a dandy test case in Tennessee, to challenge the Anti-evolution law."

"Go on," I said.

"I know a fellow, John Scopes is his name, and he teaches high school science. I think I can convince him to be the one to break the law."

"Why do you think he'll accept?"

"Because the Fundies don't like him and he doesn't like them."

"Why don't the Fundies like him?"

"He smokes cigarettes and dances," Rappelyea said.

That was good enough for me! I said I would subsidize a case testing the law, and vowed to pour all of my energies behind it. Rappelyea was dispatched to Dayton to get Scopes arrested.

LI

John Scopes was a sandy-haired, freckle-faced bump-kin. He was indicted for breaking the Anti-evolution law. This case might have remained a localized issue, if not for the intervention of Mr. Bryan. His decision to aid the prosecution turned the whole thing into a national event.

I was quite pleased.

But to counter Bryan, we had to find another name with marquee value. There was only one possibility— Clarence Darrow, the most famous trial lawyer and free thinker in the country.

He accepted.

LII

Who was Darrow, really?

It's hard to say. I think he was genuinely concerned with the plight of people. That's a fault, but one I begrudged him. What mattered was that he was an atheist and a courtroom genius. He would be the perfect match for Bryan.

The two had clashed before on this issue, in the pages of the *Chicago Tribune*. A couple of years earlier Darrow had, in a letter to that paper, challenged Bryan to answer fifty questions on the scientific reliability of Scripture. At that time, Bryan refused to be drawn into a debate on the trustworthiness of the Bible and would not answer the questions.

If only he could be forced into answering them, I thought. But there seemed to be no way to get Bryan into that position. After all, he was the prosecuting attorney. He would never take the stand and subject himself to cross-examination by the trial magician Darrow.

Never in a million, evolutionary years, I thought.

LIII

I made sure there was a carnival atmosphere in Dayton, Tennessee.

Arthur Garfield Hays and I hired a few theatrical students from New York to travel down there and pose as religious rubes. I commissioned them to paint signs and placards and hand them out around town in the days preceding the trial. They read:

Read Your Bible.

God Is Love.

Read Your Bible for a Week.

You Need God in Your Business.

Where Will You Spend Eternity?

Hell Is in the High Schools.

Devilution Is Wrong.

Ah, what the reporters would do with all this! I knew, absolutely, that they would provide just the sort of publicity I craved. For some reason, journalists were always willing puppets for my bidding. I wonder if there is something inherent in that profession that makes them so gullible.[39]

My star reporter, of course, was H. L. Mencken, whose expenses I picked up.

LIV

What of William Jennings Bryan?

I had to prepare him as well. The man was dangerous, having a rock solid faith in the Rock of Ages. If he had a chink to exploit it was pride, pride in his position as the spokesman for the entire Fundamentalist movement.

That is why I posed as a retired minister and managed to get an interview with him a few weeks before the trial.

"You are our last, best hope," I said to him.

"I shall do my best for the cause," he answered.

"The evolutionists are so powerful, so numerous. If only this case could shut them off forever!"

"That is our goal, though we must acknowledge they will be around for a long time to come."

"But one bold move on your part, Mr. Bryan, could save the day."

"What sort of move?"

"Well I was just thinking, Mr. Bryan, if you had a chance to defend the Bible from the witness stand…"

"Such a move would be highly unorthodox," he said, though I saw contemplation behind the eyes. "And I doubt that Mr. Darrow would allow that."

"But if he did, wouldn't that be a wonderful opportunity?"

"Wonderful, yes," he said.

"Well if it happens, please don't let him trick you into a scientific debate. Stick with the Bible. Against God's Word no attack can succeed!"

"Amen," said William Jennings Bryan.

LV

The trial itself would have been a quiet affair were it not for a ruling by the judge.

I doubt many fireworks would have gone off under normal circumstances. Scopes would have been convicted and the conviction appealed. That was our strategy at the ACLU.

I, of course, wanted more. I wanted a public relations victory. But it seemed I would not get it. Darrow was prepared to call several scientific witnesses, who would then be cross-examined by Bryan, and the whole thing would go to the jury.

But the judge ruled against Darrow's experts. He ruled they could not testify.

Darrow was enraged. "The state of Tennessee doesn't rule the world yet!" he exploded.

"I hope you do not mean to reflect on the court," the judge said.

"Well," answered Darrow, "you can always hope."

For that, the judge cited Darrow with contempt.

But the fact remained that the heart of the defense was cut out. Science would not get a chance to testify. So, citing fair play, Darrow asked if William Jennings Bryan would take the stand on the only subject left—the Bible.

LVI

William Jennings Bryan took the stand.

A hush fell upon the tiny courtroom, as if everyone knew history was about to be made. How eagerly I anticipated this exchange. Now, finally, we would rip the Bible apart for all the world to see.

My eager anticipation, however, was soon deflated. From the transcript itself, I convey the following:

Q. *[By Mr. Darrow]* Do you claim that everything in the Bible should be literally interpreted?

A. I believe everything in the Bible should be accepted as it is given there; some of the Bible is given illustratively. For instance: "Ye are the salt of the earth." I would not insist that man was actually salt.

Q. But when you read that Jonah swallowed the whale—or that the whale swallowed Jonah— excuse me, please—how do you literally interpret that?

A. When I read that a big fish swallowed Jonah— it does not say whale—

Q. Doesn't it? Are you sure?

A. That is my recollection of it. A big fish, and I believe it, and I believe in a God who can make a whale and can make a man and make both do what He pleases.

Q. Now, you say, the big fish swallowed Jonah, and he there remained how long—three days— and then he spewed him upon the land. You believe that the big fish was made to swallow Jonah?

A. I am not prepared to say that; the Bible merely says it was done.

Q. You don't know whether it was the ordinary run of fish, or made for that purpose?

A. You may guess; you evolutionists guess.

Q. But when we do guess, we have a sense to guess right.

A. But do not do it often.

Q But do you believe God made such a fish and that it was big enough to swallow Jonah?

A. Yes, sir. Let me add: One miracle is just as easy to believe as another.

Q It is for you.

A. It is for me.

Q. Just as hard?

A. It is hard to believe for you, but easy for me. A miracle is a thing performed beyond what man can perform. When you get beyond what man can do, you get within the realm of miracles; and it is just as easy to believe in the miracle of Jonah as any.

I was not pleased with the way things had begun. Darrow seemed overly contemptuous, and Bryan was handling himself well. At this point I jotted a note to myself: "See Mencken."

Darrow continued to hammer away at Bryan, covering Joshua and the age of the earth, but without making a dent. Suddenly, our co-counsel, Mr. Stewart, objected. "Your Honor," he said, "we are attaining no evidence."

"These gentlemen have not had much chance," Bryan said. "They did not come here to try this case. They came here to try revealed religion. I am here to defend it, and they can ask me any question they please."

The audience broke out into applause. This was not a good turn of events.

Then Darrow piped up. "Great applause from the bleachers."

"From those whom you call 'yokels,' " Bryan said.

"I have never called them yokels."

"That is, the ignorance of Tennessee, the bigotry."

"You mean who are applauding you?"

"Those are the people whom you insult."

Then Darrow lost his cool. "You insult every man of science and learning in the world because he does not believe in your fool religion!"

At that, the judge pounded his gavel. "I will not stand for that," he said. After some more argument, he allowed the questioning to continue.

Q. *[By Mr. Darrow]* Mr. Bryan, do you believe that the first woman was Eve?

A. Yes.

Q. Do you believe she was literally made out of Adam's rib?

A. I do.

Q. Did you ever discover where Cain got his wife?

A. No, sir; I leave the agnostics to hunt for her.

Q. You have never found out?

A. I have never tried to find out.

Q. You have never tried to find out?

A. No.

Q. The Bible says he got one, doesn't it? Were there other people on earth at that time?

A. I cannot say.

Q. You cannot say. Did that ever enter your consideration?

A. Never bothered me.

Q. There were no others recorded, but Cain got a wife.

A. That is what the Bible says.

Q. Where she came from you do not know. All right.

Such was Darrow's method throughout the rest of the examination. His tone was condescending, and his words crafted to convey small victories at every turn. It was not successful. Darrow came off as rather petty, and every now and then would spout something bigoted which, though I agreed with the sentiment, did not score points with the judge or public.

Once, when the audience applauded an answer by Bryan, Darrow commented, "I wish I could get a picture of these clackers."

The day wore on, and both men appeared tired. Toward the end, Bryan said, "Your Honor, I think I can shorten this testimony. Mr. Darrow's sole purpose is to slur the Bible, but I will answer his challenge. I will answer it all at once, and I have no objection in the world, I want the world to know that this man, who does not believe in a God, is trying to use a court in Tennessee—"

"I object to that!" Darrow fumed.

"—to slur at it, and while it will require time, I am willing to take it."

"I object to your statement," Darrow cried, pounding his fist on the table. "I am examining you on your fool ideas that no intelligent Christian on earth could believe."

The judge adjourned the session. I put my head in my

hand. Darrow did not "crush" William Jennings Bryan, as we had hoped.[40]

I immediately went to Mencken and said, "We have to do something."

"I'm ahead of you, professor," he said. "Leave it to me. I will write it up so that the American people will see it just as we want them to see it."

And he did.

Mencken labeled the Fundamentalists "simian gabble" and "anthropoid rabble." We all thought that was very funny.

Of Bryan, he wrote: "He is, in fact, a charlatan, a mountebank, a zany without sense or dignity. His career has brought him into contact with the first men of his time; he prefers the company of rustic ignoramuses. He seems only a poor clod like those around him, deluded by a childish theology, full of an almost pathological hatred of all learning, all human dignity, all beauty, all fine and noble things. He is a peasant come home to the barnyard."

Ah, no skeptic alive could write like Mencken. By the time the trial was finished, the impression was that Bryan had been badly defeated, in spite of the fact that John T. Scopes was found guilty![41]

LVII

I read reports that Darrow did not feel triumphant about his public victory over William Jennings Bryan. I suppose the writers, most of whom were not there, wished to paint Darrow as a paragon of objective virtue who took no glory in the tearing down of another man.

But I was there, and I can tell you Darrow loved every moment of it.[42]

Four days after the trial ended, William Jennings Bryan consumed a large meal, lay down for a nap, and died. His passing was not mourned by any of us at the ACLU.

You might also say that Fundamentalism, at least as far as the American people were concerned, died with him. It had been laughed at, mocked, and now was shunted aside by the intellectual elite of American culture. How I loved the intellectual elite! They had their own religion, the love of the self, which made them easy to manipulate.

And then, on the eve of my greatest triumph, on the border of ultimate victory, I was thrown by a series of incidents into a whirlwind of uncertainty, a maelstrom of apprehension, dismay and dread.

Locked in the storage room beneath the studio, I spent a pleasant hour with Geraldo Rivera. To some, this may seem an oxymoron, but he regaled me with war stories, ending with his interview with Charles Manson. I told him Charles Manson was a perfect consequence of evolutionary philosophy. If it weren't for a cleaning man looking for a lost mop, I might have been able to develop that theory even further.

Geraldo had a show to do. I had a manuscript to retrieve. We parted. I caught a cab to Luigi's, my favorite Italian eatery, and puzzled out some matters.

What was Brigid's motive in all this? No doubt it was about money. She had something we all valued, and was probably anxious to deliver it to the highest bidder.

Or was she? Could she have some other connection? Something about her look, her dialogue, her entire manner, set me on edge. I munched a couple of Tums and called Effie at the office.

"Jim, where have you been? I've been so worried."

"Just playing flatfoot, Effie. Any calls?"

"Several. Dundy at police headquarters. Your mother. Florence Crookshank."

"Florence? What did she want?"

"She said she just wanted to check with you to see if everything was all right."

"Oh, boy. Listen, will you drive my car out here to Luigi's? Pronto."

I downed a plate of linguini until Effie delivered my car. Then it was time for some detective work.

First stop was the offices of "Married with Children" at Fox Studios. It felt a little strange walking into a reception area strewn with giant photographs of America's most famous dysfunctional family. The eyes of Al Bundy seemed to look through me, as if to say, "Why isn't everybody as stupid as I am?"

I asked the girl at the desk if I could check their records of all talent on file. That would include anyone they'd ever seen to audition for the show.

"Now why should I allow you to see such confidential information?" the girl asked.

"Because I asked you nicely?"

"I don't think so."

"Because I once was a famous actor myself?"

Her eyes glittered slightly. "Oh? What did you do?"

"Shakespeare in New York."

"What network was that on?"

"No, the plays of William Shakespeare, staged in New York City."

"William who?"

"Shakespeare. Where'd you go to school?"

"Right here in the L.A. public school system."

"Ah."

"Ever do anything I might have seen?"

"I did a Pepsi commercial once."

"Now you look familiar! Oh, wow! Sure, what do you need to know?" She motioned me behind the desk, and tapped a few keys on her computer. We ran a name check. There was no "Brigid O'Shaughnessy."

After giving my autograph to the girl, I drove over to where "Melrose Place" is quartered. They had no record of a "Brigid O'Shaughnessy" either.

What was it about that name? Ever since she'd first said it, it struck a chord somewhere. But I couldn't figure out where. It was starting to drive me nuts.

Only one thing left to do. My shoes were getting a little dull.

"Why Mr. James Scott Bell," Chaz said, his face lighting up. "I was beginning to think I'd have to work for a living."

"Nice to see you, too, Chaz. Does the name 'Brigid O'Shaughnessy' mean anything to you?"

"How's that?" Chaz said. "I thought maybe you said somethin'."

I slipped him a ten, just to save time.

"Brigid O'Shaughnessy," Chaz said, "is the name of the character played by Mary Astor in *The Maltese Falcon.*"

"Of course!" I erupted. "And that hairdo she wore was pure Veronica Lake in *Sullivan's Travels.* I'm dealing with a movie nut who likes guns!"

"What kind of guns?"

"A Ruger .22 caliber."

"Hmm, military training pistol in the fifties. Favored by sportsmen now because of its accuracy. Very interesting, considering the going's on in Catalina."

Catalina is the little island off the Long Beach coast, long favored by the idle rich. "What's going on there?" I said.

"Dang," said Chaz, "I coulda sworn I heard some talkin'."

"Hey, I gave you a ten!"

"Mama needs an operation."

Grumbling, I fished out a five. It disappeared into Chaz's fist.

"Okay, Mr. James Scott Bell. Listen and listen good. The word on the street is Mr. Sky Tyler, the man who owns the big super station out of Louisville, is yachting on the island with his new bride, Delia Nightingale. Now what is it that first launched Mr. Sky Tyler into national prominence?"

"A movie deal, wasn't it?"

"Your name should be 'Mr. Almost Right.' Tyler bought up the film libraries of two old Hollywood studios, Paramount and Warner Brothers. He shows the movies on his super station."

"That's all very interesting, Chaz, but why should I care about what he shows?"

"Ah, the ignorance of youth. Tell me, what was Warner Brothers' biggest movie hit of 1941?"

"*Gone with the Wind.*"

"That was 1939, and a different studio, too. No, the answer is *The Maltese Falcon.*"

I said nothing, just listened to the sound of buffing on my Florsheims.

"Now that same year, what was Paramount's biggest hit?"

Swallowing, I offered, "Hope and Crosby?"

"Wrong. It was a little comedy called *Sullivan's Travels.*"

"What an incredible coincidence."

Chaz cackled. "No such thing when Chaz is talkin'. Now listen up. This one is on the house. Mr. Sky Tyler is a southern gentlemen, or likes to pretend he is, and therefore likes his bourbon and his sporting life. In fact, he is a certified marksman with a handgun, and competes all over the country. What do you think his weapon of choice is?"

"Wouldn't be a Ruger .22 caliber, would it?"

"There's hope for you yet, boy!" Chaz said. "And thank you for helping me get my kids through college."

I raced to Long Beach and nabbed the first shuttle I could to Catalina. I was going to have a little talk with Sky Tyler, and it wasn't going to be about his taste in women.

LVIII

The first incident occurred at the ACLU celebration of the Scopes "victory." We were in a private room at a midtown speakeasy. The air was redolent with the scent of knockwurst, sauerkraut and Mencken's cheap cigars. Everyone was in a happy mood, drinking beer and gin, doing Bryan imitations, and laughing it up.

Only men were present save for two women, there by special invitation.

The first woman was Margaret Sanger, coiner of the term "birth control," editor of the magazine *Woman Rebel,* founder of the National Birth Control League.[43] With her was an associate whom I only remember as "Susan."

As the evening wore on, it became rather evident that Mrs. Sanger (though she was divorced from Sanger and married to another, she retained his name) was rather put off by all the male bonding going on atop the corpse of Fundamentalism. The breaking point came when Mencken, by now thoroughly stewed, yelled across the room, "Hey Maggie! Howzabout a little birth control tonight?"

Five ACLU lawyers laughed. Margaret Sanger immediately walked over and dumped a full pint of beer on Mencken's head, effectively ending the evening's festivities.

Susan laughed at Sanger's action. I noticed and approached her.

"See here, young lady," I said. "This is outrageous."

"Ah, what's your beef, Pops?" she said. She was in her late twenties, I judged, with sparkling eyes and a curvaceous form, which she apparently took pleasure in highlighting with her clothes. A "flapper" I believe is the proper term.[44]

"Pops?" I said huffily. "Pops? Do you know to whom you are speaking?"

She took another slug of her gin. "Sir Somebody, isn't it?" She tilted back her head and giggled. That was something she would do a lot during the course of our amazing conversation.

"Sir Max Busby! And I will have you know that you would not be here if it hadn't been for my considerable influence in the history of science."

Tilt. Giggle. "Oh *that*. I know all about *that*."

"You do? Then a little respect, please."

"I don't respect you. I don't respect anything about you. If it hadn't been you it would have been somebody else. The only thing that matters is that we can do what we want, when we want. That's the whole point of this evolution thing, ain't it? We're all animals, right? So let's eat, drink, and be merry and to hell with anyone else!"

This should not have come as a shock. Here, standing before me in a haze of smoke and dim lights, was a woman of my creation, a modern woman, effectively worshipping herself and throwing off all sense of traditional morality. A microcosm of my life's work! Hadn't I wanted to replace God with Self? Wasn't this Susan, this model of modernity, precisely what I wished to see?

Well, yes, except that she was refusing to pay me the proper homage, and I realized I had no philosophical way to get her to do it.

"I'll give you one thing, Pops," she went on. "You've made it all possible."

"Made what possible?"

"The vision. The dream. The day when women will be in control of the earth. It all starts with the control of the body, right? The right to contraception. Then it moves on to the right to abortion"—she said it casually—"and from there it's every woman for herself."

That was entirely logical. If the fetus was without divine dignity, why not get rid of it when one chose to do so? I had conceived (excuse my choice of words!) of this possibility long ago.

"I see you're smiling, Pops. Well, the best is yet to come."

"Tell me!"

"Okay, okay, but don't bust a gut. At your age you can't afford it." *Tilt. Giggle.* "Now think about this. Everything will be based on money."

"Money?"

"Well, things have to be based on something, don't they?"

"I suppose."

She lit a cigarette, took a deep drag, and continued,

"All right. So money will be the thing that controls things and people. We will do things completely from a costs-versus-benefits standpoint. Are you with me so far?"[45]

"Go on."

"So, we simplify everything. When things or people get to be a real drain, we simply eliminate them."

"Eliminate?"

"You know, deep six."

"What do you mean by 'real drain'?"

"Oh you know. When there is no benefit, no use."

"To whom?"

"Whoever is in control of the situation. You just take the logic of abortion and apply it at the other end."

"I don't follow."

"To people like you, Pops. The oldsters. People of the drooping flesh. Instead of wasting everybody's time and money, instead of trying to deal with all your senile meanderings, we get rid of you. How's that sound, Pops?"

The chill that came over me was not, I think, so much in what she said. Theoretically she was absolutely correct, and who was I to argue? I was trying to achieve this very thing! Evolutionary theory was always intended to do away with objective moral reality, and that's exactly what it did! Here was the proof. The woman was quite correct.

But oh, how she said it! And how she made me realize that I had created the logic of my own demise!

LIX

I was dismayed, discomfited, out of my head! At 126 years old, that is not a healthy thing to be.

Why should I have a crisis of spirit now? I wondered. For so long I had lived in the confidence of my own rationality and egocentricity. But suddenly it was as if invisible talons had gripped my soul, and I could do nothing to remove the torment. Like Prometheus, I was tortured daily, hourly, chained upon the rocks of a merciless, graceless existence.

But as bad as all this was, as frightening and fearful, it was nothing compared to what happened next!

LX

At the behest of Mr. Harry Houdini, the magician, I attended a seance.

Mr. Houdini had an interest in spiritism (as a debunker), and I had an interest in Mr. Houdini. As a popular artist of the day, Harry held the attentions of an enormous audience. I hoped to use him as a spokesman for evolutionary theory. (I could see it thus: "Not even Houdini can escape the theory of evolution!") Unfortunately, he seemed to take more delight in picking locks with keys hidden in his cheeks than in natural science.

In any event, we went to the seance held in a Victorian home on Bunker Hill, one evening in late winter. Seven others were present there, of high social standing. I marked each one as a possible recruit (the rich, the influential, the toplofty were always high on my list).

Presently we were seated around a green felt table, round and with gold fringe, as the seance medium, one Madame DeFrasso, placed her palms on the soft surface. The lights were dim, and the participants rapt.

"I call on the spirits," the gypsy woman warbled. She wore a red satin scarf on her head which, when she moved it, caused her enormous earrings to jingle. "I call upon you, O spirits, tonight!"

I felt Harry tighten in the chair next to me. He was a

skeptic, though one who wanted to be convinced (he hoped against hope to contact his dead mother).

I, on the other hand, was downright adamant about the ridiculousness of the entire enterprise.

"There is one who doubts among us." The medium opened her eyes and looked directly at me. "Why do you doubt?"

All eyes around the table shot my way. Even Harry seemed to be saying, "So?"

I cleared my throat. "Because I have not been convinced," I said.

Madame DeFrasso squinted her eyes. "What would convince you?"

Without thinking, I met her challenge by saying, "Bring up the spirit of my father."

Why did I say this? I had a dual purpose. The first was to pick something I was sure she could not accomplish. But the second was that, somewhere deep in the recesses of my tired and sagging soul, I hoped that I could once more contact the man who had driven me to a life of evil, perhaps therein to find repose for my tormented spirit.

Madame DeFrasso did not hesitate. She asked me for his name, and then she closed her eyes once again and began to summon the spirit of my dead father.

Sweat began to form on my furrowed brow.

All the others joined the medium in the concentrated summons in which she was now engaged.

The room seemed to grow darker, or was it merely my failing eyes? The room seemed to grow colder, as if a chill wind from the center of all darkness and loneliness blew across the landscape of my soul.

And then, and then!

Oh, and then!

He was there! Hovering above the table! A spirit, an apparition—my father!

"Why have you brought me up?" he said.[46]

As I sat frozen, heart pounding like a riveter's hammer, Madame DeFrasso said, "Your son does not believe!"

And then the spirit of my father looked upon my face! "Thomas, Thomas!" he wailed.

Someone in the room screamed. Someone else collapsed onto the floor. I simply sat there, hoping my life would not be sucked from my feeble body.

"Turn back!" my father said. *Turn back!* I remembered that morning on the Thames, a lifetime ago, when those words had come to me in the fog—it had been my father!

"Thomas, it is all true!" My father's face was twisted in torment.

"What is true, Papa?" I said.

"The wrath of God!"

Oh, the chill that set upon my bones! I was sure I was going directly to eternal flames that very instant!

"Save yourself!" my father said. "Turn back!"

He began to dematerialize.

"Papa!" I cried.

"Turn back..." he said as he became a vapor, and then a void.

Madame DeFrasso reeled in her chair, earrings playing an eerie tune. My own head began to spin like a globe, into the outer darkness of an infinite universe where there was no light, no consciousness.

LXI

When I awoke, I was looking into the angelic face of a young nurse.

"We've been having quite a sleep," she said.

"Where am I?" I said.

"The hospital. You've had a shock."

All of it came back to me, the seance, my father. "You're not just whistling Dixie," I said.

"You rest now. The worst is over, thank the Lord."

Her words startled me, but in a completely new way. Normally, if anyone ever mentioned an appellation of the divine, I would react with sarcasm or scorn. But now I felt simple relief. And curiosity.

"May I ask you a question?" I said.

"Certainly."

"Do you believe in God?"

The nurse blinked, and then smiled. "Of course."

"Why?"

"I have always felt His presence, even as a little girl. He's as real to me as you are."

"But what about evolution? What about the fact of man's descent from lower forms of life?"

She chuckled. "Oh, that's just silly."

Silly! My entire life's work described by a young nurse as "silly!" My head went light on me. But strangely, it was almost a relief, as if a huge boulder were lifted from my neck and shoulders, as if the sun had broken through a dark cover of cloud and shed its light upon an evanescent earth.

As she started for the door, I asked her what her name was. "Florence Crookshank," she said.

And that is how I met the saint who now cares for me in this house.

LXII

The vision of my father haunted me for weeks. Was I merely going mad? Or was it really what it seemed to be, a warning from beyond the grave?

I began thinking a lot about graves.

And about God, my enemy. I began to think things like this: What if my father's specter was a message engineered by God Himself? What if, in other words, I had just received a Western Union from the Almighty whose demise I had sworn to bring about?

One night I stood outside my modest home in the Silver Lake district of Los Angeles and looked up into the starry sky. Making a gnarled fist, I raised it toward heaven and shouted, "You'll have to do better than that! Do you hear me? You'll have to do much better! A signed telegram might do it, but not this paltry ghost stuff, oh no! You'll have to do better than that!"

I received no answer, only the rude shout of a neighbor bidding me to shut my "trap."

Florence, now my personal nurse, was a curiosity to me. She went about her business with a pleasantness I had scarcely seen in my long sojourn on earth. It was as if an inner peace of remarkable dimension was her permanent companion. The contrast between her disposition and mine was stark. I was what the kids called a "miserable old coot."

But further misery was to come. And this time, it came over that most modern of technological advances, the radio.

Catalina was shrouded in fog as the sun set. There were a few yachts in the harbor, but Sky Tyler's wasn't hard to spot. It was the big one called "My Ego."

From shore, I hopped a water taxi out to the yacht. It was covered with festive lights, and well-heeled folks were milling around on deck, trying to look as if they had film deals or something.

A burly steward stopped me at the ladder. "You have an invitation?" he asked.

"No invitation necessary," I said. "I am Jim Bell, the famous Los Angeles attorney. You may have read about me?"

"No, sir."

"Seen me on the evening news?"

"I'm afraid not."

"Hmm. Have you heard about the O. J. Simpson murder trial?"

"Who hasn't?"

"Well, I didn't have anything to do with that, but I have a Simpson trading card."

"I'm afraid you'll have to leave, sir."

"Not so fast," I said quickly. "Tell Sky Tyler I want to see him. Tell him I have a message for Brigid O'Shaughnessy, from the fat lady."

That got his attention. He left and returned two minutes later. "Mr. Tyler will see you," he said. I told the taxi cab to keep the motor running.

Snaking his way through the moneyed minions, the steward ushered me downstairs into the master's quarters. It was a chandeliered affair, complete with plush furnishings and people who looked as if they belonged. In the plushest chair, adorned with skipper's hat and cigar, sat Sky Tyler. Directly next to him, lounging on a divan in a sparkling evening dress, was Delia Nightingale. Her "peek-a-boo" hair was just as I'd remembered it. Looking around, I noticed the steward had taken a position next to the door, as if to stop the quick exit of some fleeing soul. His gun made a noticeable bulge in his sport jacket.

"Hi, Brigid." I said. "I mean Delia."

She nodded at me. "How'd you figure it out?"

"I had a little help, though I should have been suspicious when you offered me a ride at DuPars. How would you know I didn't have a car unless you followed me there? You had me in your sights all the way from Palmdale, didn't you?"

"I knew you'd lead me to the manuscript," she said. "You didn't disappoint me."

"She's one heck of a little actress, isn't she?" said Tyler. "Now I understand you have a message for me. I'm a man in a hurry."

"I believe you have something that is rightfully mine," I said. "I'd like it back."

A smile curled across Tyler's mustachioed lip. "I have a great many things, Mr. Bell, some of which have taken me a long time to acquire. Whatever would induce me to turn anything that I have over to you?"

"A sense of right and wrong," I said. "A sense of decency."

"Ha. I quit believing in right and wrong and decency the moment I decided to get into television. It seemed like a prudent career move."

"And you, a southerner!"

"Decency was of the old South, Mr. Bell. It didn't work then, and it won't work now."

"I wonder what will work for you come Judgment Day?"

"My motto is, 'The one who dies with the most toys wins.' "

"Yeah? Mine is, 'The one who dies with the most toys is dead.' "

We stared at each other for a long moment. Then Tyler said, "And it's the religious nuts who want to take away all of my fun."

Nodding, I said, "So that's why you took the manuscript."

"What do you know about it?"

"It's starting to make sense. I can't be completely sure, but I'll give it a shot. You're planning some sort of television extravaganza, and the manuscript is going to play a central role. It's going to be a scientific show, the kind they always show on public television where they pretend recent discoveries have proven evolution true or Christianity false. My instinct is you're going to try to debunk the manuscript, with the help of one large lady. How am I doing?"

"Two tacos short of a combination plate," said a voice. The voice was followed by Hillary Horton Malloy, who stepped into the room along with Joel Nairobi and Wilmer the gun boy.

In Malloy's sausage-like fingers was the Busby manuscript.

"You think," Malloy said, "that I'd allow a manuscript like this to continue to exist? Tonight, at a small ceremony for a few invited guests, we shall burn this manuscript and dance around the flames."

The thought of that made my neck hairs snap to attention. I had to stall, but how? I fell back on the only professional skill I, a member of the bar, had at my immediate disposal—I began to talk. "The truth doesn't interest you, I suppose."

"The truth is a tool for those who control the media," Tyler said. "It can be manipulated as we please."

"This is what atheism is all about, right?" I asked Hillary Horton Malloy. "No basis for truth at all. If there is no God, anything is permissible. And anything is believable."

"Atheism will rule the world," said Malloy.

"You're playing on a losing team," I said. "You and your kid."

"Just keep it up," said Wilmer.

"Shut up, Wilmer," said Malloy.

"Don't tell me to shut up!"

"Shut up!"

"That's it," I said. "Complete chaos. The only outcome possible for atheistic thieves." Turning to Wilmer, I said, "Five to ten they sell you out when it comes time for the cops to pick a fall guy."

Wilmer's face almost let off steam, but then he turned to Malloy and said, "What's he talking about?"

"Shut up, Wilmer," said Malloy.

"I'll tell you, Wilmer," I said quickly. "Atheism can't account for moral values, which means they can turn you over to the cops and not miss a minute of sleep over it!"

"Enough!" shouted Tyler.

"I'll say when it's enough!" shouted Wilmer.

"Not on my ship, you won't!"

Nairobi whined, "Please, my head is splitting."

"I wonder what your head will do," I said, "when you find out Wilmer here sold the manuscript to Geraldo Rivera."

Delia shouted at Wilmer, "You fool!"

"Go stand in the corner!" Malloy shouted at Wilmer.

"Oh, yeah!" Wilmer pulled out a revolver and pointed it at his mother. "Well *I've had it*, you hear me? I've had it! 'Wilmer do this, Wilmer do that! Wilmer kill this guy, Wilmer kill that guy!' I'm pulling out! I'm going out on my own! I'm gonna get on TV myself, with Geraldo and 'Hard Copy' and anyone else who'll have me. Yeah, that's it! Me, Wilmer Malloy! And Tom Cruise will play me in the movie!"

A chilly silence gripped the chamber.

"He's crazy," Tyler said.

"Give me the manuscript!" Wilmer shouted at his mother.

"Now, Wilmer, don't do anything rash," said Malloy.

"I'll have a rash if I want to! I'm fed up! Hand it over or I'll blow a hole through you! And nothing can stop me."

"Listen to reason, son!"

I piped, "What reason? Wilmer's right. If he has a gun, and God does not exist, he's in control."

"Yeah!" Wilmer squealed, his eyes darting crazily from side to side. "Now give it!"

"I do believe he's serious," I said.

Malloy slowly handed Wilmer the Busby manuscript. He smiled, then said, "Don't anybody move!"

Nobody did. We waited for Wilmer's next move, which just happened to be downward. He was trying to back out of the room when he tripped over a jockey statuette. His gun went off, killing the lights. Delia screamed as everything went dark.

Sky Tyler shouted, "Get him!"

In the blackness and confusion, I dove in the general direction of Wilmer Malloy. I felt bodies and shoes and breath around me. My arms flailed wildly in an attempt to find the manuscript. To my surprise, I grabbed a handful of paper. Rolling backward, I scrambled to my feet, found the door, and escaped.

"Get him!" I heard Tyler scream. This time I knew it was for me.

I chugged down a narrow passage, hit the stairs at full tilt, and banged my knee. Scrambling up to the main deck, I bumped through the moneyed carousers on my way toward the water taxi.

The cap had the motor idling, just as I'd asked him to. Scuttling down to my boat, I screamed, "Hit it!"

We shot out toward shore. Looking back, I saw a knot of confused atheists make like the Keystone Kops at the rail. "Some party," the cap said. "Sounds like they're having a great time."

"They're jumping for joy, I imagine," I said. For fifty bucks the guy took me across the channel himself. As we headed into the night I leaned back on the rails and slowly let out a breath. Soon, the sounds from the party gave way to the lapping of water against the hull. "Thank you, Lord," I whispered.

By midnight I was in my office.

LXIII

Aimee Semple McPherson had risen like a lumines-cent moon over the planet of fundamentalism. She revolved around the landscape of urban America, casting her light upon the unsaved masses. She had founded what she called the "International Church of the Foursquare Gospel," built upon the four roles of Jesus Christ—savior, baptizer, healer, and coming king.

I would not have noticed her much, save for three salient facts.

First, she built a huge worship center in the middle of Los Angeles, at a cost of over $1.5 million, which she called Angelus Temple. This was no small feat for a woman in 1923.

Second, she founded a radio station, and her mel-lifluous voice was piped to millions.

Third, and most important from my perspective, she used her position and fame to argue, in the most strident of terms, against the truth of evolution! Here is where I began to draw a line.

How well I remember that night when I happened to tune the radio to a debate between Mrs. McPherson and the atheist Lee Hubris Mellon. The latter was a colleague of mine, a brilliant debunker of Christianity, and founder of the American Association for the Advancement of Atheism (the "Four A"). I had, at one time, staked him some funds so he could begin his work. Now he took full advantage of his turn at the microphone:

"Ladies and gentlemen," he began, "I wish to thank the generous, though seriously misguided, Mrs. McPherson for the opportunity to address you tonight. I hope you shall not take offense if my speech fails to indulge my hostess with the benefit of any doubt. For there is no doubt, my friends, that the Bible is a fraud, an unscientific collection of ancient myths, and that modern science has truly found the source of our existence, and it is very simply this: nothing. Yes my friends, we were hatched by chance in a blind universe, and we must make the best of it, with manly courage and good sense."

Gleefully, I leaned in closer to the radio. I gloried in the rest of Mellon's talk, which hit all the right notes.

And then a golden voice took to the air—confident, clear, mesmerizing. Sister Aimee's voice, which began, "Mr. Chairman, Honorable Opponent, Ladies and Gentlemen. When first I found I was to debate Lee Hubris Mellon, knowing he had debated with the outstanding fundamental ministers of the United States of America, I was fearful lest I could not hold up my end of the debate. But I knew that the Bible could stand any test. It is like the great Rock of Gibraltar. Waves may beat against it. Atheists, agnostics, and higher critics may pile up the waters against it; but they fall back, breathing out their own futility, and the Rock of Ages still stands. So, because of the Bible, I no longer had any fear."

I felt myself gripping the armrests of my chair with all the might left in my feeble fists. Something about her was so confident! It was as if she reached through the airwaves with long arms of sound, shaking the doubters and assuring them she had the truth, the whole truth, and nothing but the truth!

She continued: "I had no desire, in accepting the challenge, to defend the Bible because the Bible needs no defense. Should I see a little boy making spitballs and popping them up at the sun, and saying, 'O Sun, I will put you out,' I wouldn't feel called upon to protect the sun. The sun will be shining when the little boy is gone and forgotten. If I should see a lad with his bucket down at the edge of the Pacific dipping up water and saying, 'Old Ocean, I am going to empty you," I would not call on the police to come down and protect the ocean from the little boy. It is bigger than he. And, thank God, the Bible and God and faith and hope and love and truth and charity are greater than all the atheistic ravings of the world!"

Sustained applause followed. It was clear, very clear to me at that moment, that I was hearing the greatest threat to my mission I had ever encountered. Radio, and this woman, and others to come, could so propagandize the masses that they would no longer know who to believe.

This lady preacher awakened me from my melancholy. She was all I needed to refuel the passion of my life's purpose. After Scopes, I was sure the demise of Creationism was near. Now, I could no longer afford to be sanguine. One Sister Aimee, loosed upon the land through the miracle of radio, could be the vehicle to undo in a single season what had taken me nearly a century to accomplish!

The seeds of a final, grand plan began to take root in me. It was a decidedly wicked idea, for not only would it stop Sister Aimee, it would prove a warning for all who dared to imitate her.

LXIV

It was time to cash in some promises. Lee Hubris Mellon had long consorted with various low forms of life. Being an atheist, he saw no long-term consequences in this, and the criminal element was sometimes useful to him in his efforts on behalf of intimidating Christians. I was thus able to obtain from him the name of a Los Angeles mobster, known only to me as "Steve," and met with him at a dark noodle restaurant in the heart of Chinatown.

He was around forty, a stocky man, and he wore a brown suit and a fedora. He'd brought with him a fellow he called "Jake," a tall, bony lout with a gold tooth.

"I understand you're a man who likes to do business," I said.

"If the reward outweighs the risk," Steve said.

"How does $1 million sound?"

"Keep talking."

I did. And he listened. Jake smiled silently throughout, his gold tooth reflecting the light of the street lamp outside.

LXV

On May 18, 1926, Aimee Semple McPherson took her customary trip to the beach at Ocean Park, along with her secretary, one Emma Schaffer. She liked to go there to work on her sermons. This day she did not know she was being watched.

Sister Aimee did some scribbling under a beach tent, for what seemed an eternity. Finally, her secretary withdrew to a nearby drugstore, and Aimee Semple McPherson went for a swim.

One thing that was certain about the revivalist was her immense popularity as a healer. She was often collared by suffering citizens who bade her make intercession for themselves or their loved ones.

So it would not have been strange for Sister Aimee, while wading in the Pacific surf, to be confronted by a desperate-looking woman sobbing, "Our baby is dying, Sister! The doctor has given it up. We've come all the way from Altadena to have you pray for the child. Please come to our car!"

No, this would not have seemed strange in the least, nor would Sister Aimee's willing compliance. What was out of the ordinary was that when she got to the car she did not find a sickly infant but rather a gold-toothed man, who pulled her inside the automobile and chloroformed her into unconsciousness.

LXVI

We had secured a shack just south of Agua Prieta, Mexico. Here is where Aimee Semple McPherson awakened to a quartet of strange faces—Steve and Jake, of course, the woman who had importuned her at the beach (and who was called, improbably, "Mexicali Rose"), and yours truly.

The surface plan was simple—ransom. I would leave that to Steve and his cohorts. My purpose was to frighten Sister Aimee into submission, get her to renounce her stand on evolution, and if unsuccessful in this see to it that she met an untimely but highly publicized demise.

So as Steve, Jake and Mexicali Rose, prepared their ransom demands, I set to work on the twisting of Sister Aimee's soul.

One day, as the others were out for supplies, I sat across from the bound preacher and, as the Americans say, laid it on the line.

"You will stop preaching against evolution," I said. "Is that clear?"

She seemed, at first, surprised. "Is that why I have been brought here?"

"In part."

"Your part?"

"Yes."

"And what is your interest in evolution?"

Tapping the rotting wooden floor with my cane, I said, "Suffice to say that it is my life's passion, and people like you are my life's pain. I intend to deal with both right now."

Suddenly, a look came into her eyes that I can only describe as "knowing." It was as if she could see into me, and understood every sinew of my enfeebled body, every secret of my decrepit mind.

"I take it you're not a Christian," she said.

"Ha!"

"Would you laugh at God?"

"I've spent my life doing just that, young woman."

"You should know one thing then."

"What is that?"

"God is not laughing. He is crying, crying for a lost soul who will not come home."

"Home indeed! Between God and myself there is a fixed separation, and it shall never be bridged!"

Sister Aimee seemed suddenly radiant. Her next words I recognized as Holy writ. "Who shall separate us from the love of Christ? Shall tribulation, or distress, or persecution, or famine, or nakedness or sword?"

"That will be enough," I said.

"As it is written, for thy sake we are killed all the day long; we are accounted as sheep for the slaughter. Nay, in all these things we are more than conquerors through Him that loved us."

"I said enough!"

"For I am persuaded, that neither death, nor life, nor angels, nor principalities, nor powers, nor things present, nor things to come, nor height, nor depth, nor any other creature, shall be able to separate us from the love of God, which is in Christ Jesus our Lord. "

"Stop!" I tried mightily to hide my trembling, without success. I stood up and shuffled slowly to the evangelist. Hovering, I said, "I'm afraid, Mrs. McPherson, that you will have to die here."

LXVII

Steve said, "She ain't afraid to die, eh? We'll see about that."

The ransom demand had run into trouble. Minnie, Aimee's mother, was asking for proof that we indeed had her daughter.

"I'll lop off a hunk of her hair," Mexicali Rose said. "And if that doesn't work, maybe we'll send a finger."

Throughout this ordeal, Sister Aimee sat impassively. She had more courage than I'd seen in a thousand men before her. Apparently, she truly believed in her Savior.

When I next had a chance to be with her alone, she said, "I don't believe your heart is in this venture."

"Do not be deceived," I answered.

"So if I am to die, I feel that I can ask you for one last request."

"Last request?"

Sister Aimee said, "I am wearing a necklace. It's not much, but it was a gift from my mother and means so much to her. Will you take it please and see that she gets it?"

I was not sure why I took it. I was a nihilist, one who did not live with any ultimate meaning in mind. Perhaps I thought this simple act on behalf of a kidnap victim could not possibly matter, one way or the other. Maybe I was just

curious. Whatever the reason, I strode to the roped revivalist, reached under her collar and pulled a silver chain from
around her neck. A tiny item bobbed on the chain. And
that's when my heart almost stopped beating.

For there, dangling from my hands, was a crude angel
figure fashioned from dark ironstone, the only one of its
kind.

"Where did you get this?" I demanded.

"It was a gift from my mother. Why?"

"Never mind why. Where did she get it?"

"She told me she found it in a little pawn shop in
London. She thought it would always help me remember
I'm protected by angels."

I staggered.

"Does this remind you of something?" Sister Aimee
asked.

"Impossible..."

"You've seen one like it before, perhaps?"

Mind reeling, I pondered the odds against such an
impudent slap from the hand of fate. It was too much of a
strain, so I quit pondering. Instead, I began to mumble.
"I...I...this...this belonged to me at one time in my life.
How can it be? What are the chances?"

As my voice trailed off I noticed Sister Aimee's eyes
suddenly glistening. She smiled, as if in recognition of
some truth beyond my grasp and said, "Perhaps chance is
not involved at all."

"I beg your pardon?"

"Perhaps," she said, "it was designed to happen in just this way."

Stunning thought! But who was I to deny it? I was holding the blasted angel in my bony fingers!

I, who knew the incalculable odds against Darwinism being true; I, who had denied those odds to carry out my program of deceit; I, who had turned my back resolutely against the workings of Divine Providence; I, Sir Max Busby, enemy of God, against all known odds, had received a Divine Western Union, after all.

My greatest fear at that moment was that the message had been delivered "collect."

LXVIII

I could not resist anymore.

I asked Mrs. McPherson to keep my name out of any accounts for what I was about to do.

When the others were gone on one of their many shopping trips, I opened a syrup can with a jagged edge, and said, "Sister Aimee, your freedom is nigh."

She blessed me, and bade me keep the angel which had so recently hung about her neck.

You will, no doubt, have read in the papers the account of Sister Aimee's escape. She wandered seventeen hours in the Mexican desert before collapsing on the front porch of one Ramon Gonzalez.

And so Los Angeles got back, as if from the dead, its most illustrious voice.

And I? I came back from the dead, too.

I knew they'd come, hat in hand, probably that morning. I told Effie if the little guy and the fat lady showed up, to usher them right in. Usher she did, at exactly 9:00 A.M.

"Good morning," I said cheerily. "Did you have a good time at the party?"

Hillary Horton Malloy was in no mood to swap small talk. Nairobi appeared wan and tired. I motioned for them both to sit down.

"Okay, Mr. Bell," said Malloy. "You appear to be holding the cards. I thought I'd give you one last chance to relent."

"And give you the manuscript?"

"Exactly. For a price."

"I'm afraid I can't do that."

"Oh, yes you can. And no one needs to know about our little transaction."

I took my feet off my desk and leaned forward. "No, Ms. Malloy, I can't give it to you because I don't have it."

Malloy and Nairobi gasped simultaneously.

"What do you mean you don't have it?" Nairobi said, shooting to his feet.

"I mean that as of 3:00 A.M. this morning the Busby manuscript is safely in the hands of the United Parcel Service, on its way to the offices of a book publisher up north. The saga is over."

Nairobi began to pant. He turned toward the fat lady and said in a low snarl, "You bungler! You bloated idiot!" Then he burst into tears.

The fat lady just sat there looking, it seemed to me, into her immediate future. "Well," she said finally. "There are other ways. This isn't over, Mr. Bell, not by a long shot. The destruction of religion will come later if not sooner, and this episode will only be a brief blip on the screen."

"We'll see," I said.

"I could kill you right now," said Malloy.

"You won't."

"Why not?"

"Because it wouldn't be in your best interest, and everything you do is in your best interest. All the facts are in a sworn statement in my safety deposit box. If anything happens to me the police will get it, and your little empire will be in serious jeopardy. No, you aren't about to let one small lawyer ruin a vast plan for the takeover of the culture."

"But as I said, there are other ways. I have powerful friends."

"Like Sky Tyler?"

"Yes. And the best is yet to come."

She stood then and said, "Come on, Joel. Are we going to let a little setback get us down, or are we going to go take over the world?"

Nairobi sighed.

"And you, Mr. Bell," said Hillary Horton Malloy. "I suspect I may run into you again."

"If I'm doing something right, you probably will."

With a laugh like an evil queen, Malloy left my office, followed by the little Moroccan. The scent of gardenia lingered for awhile, like a bad dream.

LXIX

I was frequently confined to a wheelchair, and lovely Florence would take me for a "spin" when the weather was nice. She must have sensed something amiss with me, for she kept trying to cheer me up. I put her off, saying things like, "Just drive."

It was on a sunny Sunday morning that Florence— my sweet, innocent caretaker—played a dastardly trick upon this frail old man.

The sun was warm and pleasant, and I nodded off in the chair as we wheeled down the boulevard. I dreamed of angels then, a horde of them, smiling and nodding in my direction, wings flapping in some anticipatory frolic.

When I awoke, I was in a strange and ominous place. There were people there, and a sound, an eerie sound, ushering from huge pipes on the wall. Colored windows surrounded me. I gasped, and looked for Florence. She was next to me, patting my hand.

And then she stood up, with all the other people, and began to sing.

A mighty fortress is our God.

A bulwark never failing.

Our helper He amid the flood

Of moral ills prevailing.

Church! I was in church on Sunday morning!

I wanted to scream, get out of there, but I couldn't make a sound. I was…listening. Listening to the singing, to the words…

The words were beautiful. I thought, *How strange.* How strange that I should be moved by such words. Strange that I should find anything beautiful at all! For how can mere accidents of nature be bound by concepts like beauty?

When the singing stopped, the preacher took the pulpit. As he began to speak, a spark of recognition illuminated within me. I knew this man, though from where I could not remember.

He took his text from the Book of Psalms. "The heavens declare the glory of God," he read. "And the firmament showeth his handiwork."

And then he looked directly at me. Eyes of confident piety he had, and a sparkle of intent, as if he had read that passage for me alone. That's when I remembered him. He was older now, but there was no doubt. He was the young preacher who had once interrupted a speech of mine, and who had pledged to pray for my welfare!

When the service ended Florence wheeled me in to meet the preacher in his study. He put out his hand and said, "Welcome."

"I know you," I stammered.

"And I knew you the moment you entered the

church. You made a deep impression on me many years ago."

"I did?"

"Indeed. And I have never ceased praying for you, as I promised."

My socks, as the young people say, were knocked off. "Why?" I asked. "Why should you do such a thing for all these years?"

"It is God's desire that none should perish, but that all should come to repentance."

There comes a time in every man's life when the cumulative effect of forces beyond his control begin to take their toll. For me, that time was now. I had fought my fight, and was faithful almost to the end. But God had chipped away at my armor, the burden and weight of a lifetime, and now I was ready to let it fall.

I looked at the preacher, my eyes moist with the salt tears of surrender. "What must I do to be saved?" I asked.

The preacher smiled at me. Warm and gentle was that smile, knowing and understanding. And for the first time in my long life, I became friends with a man of God.

He baptized me a few days later, in the blue Pacific. I was washed in the Blood of the Lamb. My spirit, soul, and body, ancient entities all, felt sweetly renewed, like the headwaters of a pure stream, running toward the ocean that was eternity, where the God who was once my enemy was now my Savior, and where I would spend forever and forever and forever, and where all things were created and nothing existed by chance alone.

There would be those who found my turnabout implausible, coming as it did at the end of a long, calcified life of enmity with God. I could only say to such, "Grace is a funny thing."

LXX

Word got back to Lee Hubris Mellon that I had something to do with the escape of Sister Aimee, and that I had repudiated the theory of evolution.

I went into hiding. Mellon, the leading atheist in the country, knew only too well what the stakes were. And he knew that the only inhibition to murdering an enemy of his cause was the risk of being caught. One old man would not present much of a problem in that regard. A dark night, a blow to the head, one more accident of nature removed from this mortal coil...

I needed a change of address. Florence helped me secure this residence, under a false name, and I began to scribe this manuscript.

Several times, too tired to go on, I was tempted to stop. I feared for my life, wondering which way was up. But whenever these feelings came over me, I would look at the small angel sitting on my writing desk, and be reminded of the protection of heavenly hosts. Even for an old sinner like me.

And I would think of poor Darwin, of Huxley, of Darrow and Scopes, of the myriad figures throughout this sordid history who used and misused an interesting but misguided notion about the origin of species.

I would remember my father and wonder about the demons that drove him to so misrepresent the God who had made him. I'd think of Willie, of compassion, of Sister Aimee and my preacher friend. What was it he once told me? "God works out everything into a pattern for good for those who love him."

The great Pattern Maker had proven Himself through the tapestry of my own life. I owed Him everything.

And so I continued to write.

LXXI

My account is now finished.

What I began, however, continues to gather momentum. Evolutionary thinking is taking over the collective mind of the culture. This is as I'd planned.

My prayer is that this manuscript, when placed in the right hands, will turn men's hearts back to their true Source.

You who read these words, know this: The theory of natural descent was driven by the desire to overthrow the preeminence of the Creator God! We knew what we wanted, and that was to vanquish the Church. We wished to establish ourselves as the new priests of a secular religion.

You see, it is all about power. I know that now. It is about the infernal desire of men to wrest control from the established Authority and set up their own version of the truth.

This is what the Bible teaches about the nature of man. I am living proof.

It takes courage to oppose the theory of evolution. You are cast against the claims of "objective science." You are scorned by those with fancy titles and a command of scientific aracana and theoretical jargon. You must recognize there is no objectivity here, but a set of conclusions which flow from a premise that is held by faith alone, a premise that holds there is no God, no supernatural.

If you would oppose evolution, do so with all the force you have, for the stakes are the highest of all—the eternal resting place of our souls.

My time is almost near. Yours shall be here sooner than you think. Take heed, then, from the Voice of Voices, issuing across the millennia: "He that has ears to hear, let him hear."

So ends the manuscript.

Sir Max Busby died February 12, 1927, exactly 128 years from the date of his birth.

But his legacy remains. In his manuscript we possess a singular account of the Darwin conspiracy, which exposes for all the driving force behind this "war" of ideas. Sir Max would have approved of the following quotation from the *Columbia History of the World,* chapter 61, "Science Versus Theology":

Science and theology are rivals, because each professes to supply mankind with a comprehensive account of the universe, including man and his deepest concerns. It is true that scientists often disclaim this large intention and assert that natural science (or, as it was called until about 1850, natural philosophy) deals only with inanimate things and is silent about the realm of consciousness which is man's. But this dividing line is not in fact respected. A science of living things and a science of man are goals actively pursued by the scientific mind from its earliest impulse toward universal knowledge; and so soon as "natural philosophy" boasts that its method holds a monopoly of tested, "objective" truth, it is inevitable that every great scientific advance should bring with it direct application to man and society. At the least, "implications are drawn" in domains other than that of brute matter, which means supplanting the existing theological or philosophical teachings.

Sir Max recognized this dynamic. His narrative thus points us to the inevitable conclusion—this is all a battle for the soul. And the choices we make, the alliances we form, have consequences that are everlasting.

Now you have read it. I have done my part to carry out Sir Max's wishes. What will you do with the information now that you have it? I cannot add anything to the sage advice I received on that remarkable day a few short years ago:

Don't blow it.

Author's Note

What you have just read is based on history—names, places, and thoughts expressed. I have, by and large, employed fact, though with a fiction writer's obvious poetic license. The essentials of the history, however, are correct. (The contemporary portions of the novel, however, are completely fictitious, with no assertions of actual fact. They are the author's literary hyperbole, fancifully fair comment and satirical fabrication—nothing more).

The footnotes in the text are all factually derived. They are my winks and nods to those readers who are especially interested in the history of ideas in general, and the intellectual flummery of Darwinism in particular.

Darwin did struggle his entire life with what he had wrought. He was pulled toward religious faith by his upbringing and his wife, Emma, but he was yanked toward atheism by the implications of his theory and the zeal of his followers. The death of his young son, Charles Waring Darwin, was a blow that most certainly pushed him further along the path of doubt.

Darwin held back for years on publishing his theory, and was almost upstaged by Wallace. His friends, most notably Sir Charles Lyell, pushed the theory quickly into the forefront by way of the Linnean Society.

Most of the personages mentioned are historical. There are some obvious exceptions.

The Reverend Melville Cackle is a composite representing a strain of mainline Protestantism, the "compromising strain," where a low view of the Bible is held, if it is viewed at all.

Phillip Phatt and the young preacher who challenges Busby are fictional, as is the flapper who appears after the Scopes trial.

Harry Houdini, of course, did exist, and did frequent seances, because he held out the hope he could one day contact his departed mother. Madame DeFrasso could have been real, but that would be pure coincidence. Florence Crookshank would have made a dandy real person as well.

Aimee Semple McPherson remains a fascinating historical figure. This founder of the Foursquare Church did, indeed, disappear in May of 1926, showing up five weeks later wandering the desert at Agua Prieta, Mexico. Her abduction story, including the names Steve, Jake, and Mexicali Rose, held the headlines for weeks. Though many of the particulars of this event are still shrouded in mystery, it was simply too juicy an occurrence for this novelist to pass up. Coming the year after the Scopes trial, it fit perfectly within the narrative. Those interested in more detail may see *Sister Aimee: The Life of Aimee Semple McPherson,* by Daniel Mark Epstein. The reference to a debate on evolution is based on fact, for Sister Aimee did engage opponents in formal argumentation over the subject. Her speech is taken verbatim from just such an engagement. The atheist opponent, Lee Hubris Mellon, is a fictional character, but one I suspect will return in a future novel.

My primary authority for the sections on Charles Darwin the man was *The Survival of Charles Darwin*, by Ronald W. Clark. This was also a good source for information on Thomas Huxley and all the others in the Darwinian circle.

Evolution: The Great Debate by Vernon Blackmore and Andrew Page was an excellent source for the popular history of the theory and many of the personalities involved.

For those wishing more information on the Piltdown Man fraud, and the participation of Pierre Teilhard de Chardin, I recommend chapter 6 in Michael Pitman's *Adam and Evolution.*

The transcript and other details about the Scopes trial may be found in *A Pictorial History of the World's Great Trials* by Brandt Aymar and Edward Sagarin, and in *Attorney for the Damned,* Arthur Weinberg, editor.

General inspiration and information were drawn from one of the most important books in recent memory, *Darwin on Trial* by Phillip E. Johnson. I commend this critique of Darwinism to all who enjoyed this novel, and especially to those who did not.

About the Author

James Scott Bell studied philosophy, creative writing, and film in college, acted in Off Broadway theater in New York, and received his law degree, with honors, from the University of Southern California.

He once believed in evolution. He went to public schools.

A former trial lawyer, Bell has had two screenplays optioned for feature film production. He now writes full time in Southern California where he lives with his wife, Cindy, and their children, Nathaniel and Allegra.

The Darwin Conspiracy is his first novel.

End Notes

1. Troubled father/child relationships appear to have been present in the lives of most influential atheists— Nietzsche, Freud, and Thomas Huxley, to name three. It is clear that their atheism was less a philosophy than a neurosis. For further reflection on this phenomenon, see John Koster, *The Atheist Syndrome* (1989). —JSB

2. By this time Hemingway had written numerous short stories and two novels, to enthusiastic reviews. The letter referred to was indeed written by Hemingway's mother. Hemingway reacted with rage, and for the rest of his life harbored a deep hatred for her. See Kenneth S. Lynn, *Hemingway* (1987). In 1961, after a lifetime of trying to live according to his atheistic code of manliness, Ernest Hemingway put a double-barreled shotgun to his head and went to receive the ultimate review. —JSB

3. Sir Max recognized the heart of the issue. The Book of Genesis is the foundation point for man's meaning and existence. It sets the boundaries of his spiritual nature, and tells him where he fits into the entire creation. God, as creator, becomes the basis for all morality, all meaning. He establishes the right of revelation and law-giving. Man, the

created, has his purpose set before him—to live according to the plan of his Maker, to obey, and to glorify Him. Remove this book, and you are left with nothing to build upon but your own foundation. Indeed, it can be argued that the first question all men must deal with is this: What will you do with Genesis? —JSB

4. Busby here shows his nineteenth-century thought process by assuming that complexity in creation is something in which God would not indulge. As if, in order to be divine, creation would have to meet a man-made standard of simplicity. The same prejudice infects much "enlightened" scientific thought today. You'll often hear an evolutionist say, "Why did God choose to design the Hornbill like that? It could have been done much more efficiently." The answer, of course, is that He is God, and His efficiency is revealed in the very complexity that is beyond little minds. —JSB

5. The year 1844 proved to be momentous in other ways. That same year, Karl Marx met Friedrich Engels in Paris, laying the foundation for what became *The Communist Manifesto.* In England, George Williams formed the Young Men's Christian Association, an organization dedicated to inculcating Christian values in boys during their formative years (the Sir Max of this time would have been delighted to learn that in the 1990s atheists would sue to force the YMCA to issue them membership). Finally, 1844 was the year one of Sir Max's greatest prophets was born, the nihilist Friedrich Nietzsche. —JSB

6. The "fossil record problem" has not been cleared up. It continues to be a major obstacle for Darwinians, and

has resulted in many convoluted hypotheses. It is unlikely Sir Max fully anticipated how far ranging this problem would be. —JSB

7. Darwin was indeed troubled by these symptoms for the rest of his life. Many speculate that this was a classic inner struggle, a spiritual conflict, and that deep within the naturalist knew he had taken a leap into the dark faith of atheism, and was crying out for help. —JSB

8. Huxley, indeed, was the man. Known to history as "Darwin's Bulldog," he allowed his anti-Christian dysphoria to overpower his rational faculties. He once wrote to a colleague, "I am very glad that you see the importance of doing battle with the clericals.... I desire that the next generation may be less fettered by the gross and stupid superstitions of orthodoxy that mine has been. And I shall be well satisfied if I can succeed to however small an extent in bringing about that result." Today, numerous blather-skites are in the running for the title of lead "bulldog" (a term with, obviously, more than one meaning), the front-runner being, perhaps, Richard Dawkins, author of *The Blind Watchmaker*. —JSB

9. How ironic that today the opposite is true! When evidence accumulates and points away from the evolutionary faith, it is rejected out of hand, or twisted into forms of man's own making. —JSB

10. *Origin of Species* sent immediate shock waves of influence around the globe. As early as December 1859, Engels wrote to Marx: "Darwin, whom I am just now reading, is splendid." (See Ronald W. Clark, *The Survival*

of Charles Darwin, 230.) Darwinism thus became a corner-stone of communism. —JSB

11. Hort became the first in a long line of "compromising clergymen," who eagerly bowed to the spirit of the times with the resulting "I know not what" theology. —JSB.

12. It is remarkable how Busby anticipated the future of most discourse, relegated as it is to the use of sound bites. And, in his preparation of Huxley, he prefigured the "handlers" who are now employed by politicians to create catch phrases for their bosses to parrot. —JSB

13. These, indeed, were the exact words uttered by Wilberforce and Huxley at this momentous occasion. One cannot underestimate the power of rhetoric, a power which Huxley wielded with considerable skill. —JSB

14. Busby could not have anticipated the wild speculation that would gain scientific credibility to deal with this problem of no transitional forms. The theory of "punctuated equilibrium," created by Niles Eldredge and Stephen Jay Gould in the early seventies, postulates that we don't have transitions because evolution takes place in sudden "leaps." But in true Busby fashion, no one can explain why these leaps take place, nor describe their mechanism. It is, in other words, another aspect of evolutionary "faith." Busby would have been very happy with this theory because it allows naturalists to believe the unbelievable, and to call "fact" the non-factual. For indeed Gould and others contend to this day that "evolution is a fact," though they have no empirical data upon which to rely. —JSB

15. In 1985 two eminent scientists, Sir Fred Hoyle and Chandra Wickramasinghe, presented their case that *Archaeopteryx* was a blatant forgery. The British Museum of Natural History, which paid a pretty penny for the fossil, naturally disagrees. The curious thing is that even if *Archaeopteryx* were the "real thing," it would not make a case for descent through modification. That is because no other fossils lead to it or come from it. It is thus not an example of transformation. —JSB

16. Woodcuts of this type were a popular form of imaging at the time. Many are preserved in public domain clip art collections. —JSB

17. Haeckel, like Huxley in England, saw Darwinism as a weapon to destroy the Church. He became one of the high priests of Busby's new religion. —JSB

18. The speculation that Bölsche was an ancestor of the American actress Shirley MacLaine is without foundation, so far as I can determine. —JSB

19. Busby, of course, did not live long enough to encounter Carl Sagan, whose poetic *Cosmos* would one day attempt to impart a religious faith in a warm, fuzzy universe in which we human beings continued to evolve. —JSB

20. There is no indication Sir Max had any more interaction with Nietzsche, who became increasingly deranged in his later years. In 1889 the man who would kill God suffered a breakdown from which he never recovered, and died in an asylum in 1900. —JSB

21. Official biographers report that Darwin's last words were as Sir Max phrased them. See, e.g., Clark, op. cit. But there is historical support for the possibility that Darwin, on his deathbed, sought the solace of the religion he had abandoned. While this view is bitterly opposed by Darwin hagiographers, Sir Max's account is by no means fanciful. —JSB

22. A reference to the assassination of President James Garfield in 1881. —JSB

23. Today, Busby's "daydream" is much closer to being a reality. Parents who discipline their children according to biblical principles may be in danger of an illegal abuse charge. Religion is banned from schools and textbooks. The mere mention of God by a student or teacher may, under the right circumstances, result in expulsion. A student may use God's name profanely and it is considered free speech. But use it reverently, and it's out you go. —JSB

24. Margaret Sanger founded what we know today as Planned Parenthood of America. —JSB

25. At the time this passage was written, around 1926, Adolf Hitler was building a following for his National Socialist Party in Munich. He had served time in prison after a failed *putsch* in 1923, and while behind bars penned his manifesto, *Mein Kampf.* An early version of the manuscript makes reference to a "Vienna coffee house" conversation with a "prunelike old man" who made some "clear-headed remarks" about the threat of the Jews to the world. This passage, however, did not make it into the printed version. —JSB

26. Harvard is still a hotbed of strange theories on the law, such as Critical Legal Studies, which basically says there is no law, only the exercise of power by vicious power groups. But what about when powerless groups get power and become vicious themselves? This movement has no answer. —JSB

27. Originally published in the British satirical magazine, *Punch*. —JSB

28. Here Busby unquestioningly accepts the evolutionist's method of extrapolating an entire creature from a small bit of bone. This practice is still prevalent today. We are periodically told that a minuscule bone fragment can be taken and forged into a picture of a man-ape which usually ends up looking like the later Marlon Brando. —JSB

29. Pierre Teilhard de Chardin (1881-1955) was passionate about combining evolutionary theory with Christian faith. A "theistic evolutionist," he opined that God worked through natural descent. His enthusiasm for the project may have been motivated by a rebellion against the authority of the Vatican (which disapproved of his views). This phenomenon—man's revolt against authority—is as old as Eden, and even those who have taken priestly vows are not immune. —JSB

30. The fraud was exposed in 1953. For information on the hoax, and Teilhard's part in it, see Michael Pitman, *Adam and Evolution* (Kentwood, Mich.: Baker Book House, 1984), 91-94.—JSB

31. Sir Max did not live to see the fruition of this encounter. In 1927, Russell published his book *Why I Am*

Not a Christian. It caused a stir, but today seems a rather tired rehash of long since repudiated arguments. For one of Western civilization's notable philosophers, it is not much of a legacy. Russell spent the later years of his life (age seventy and beyond) in the pursuit of young females. Not surprisingly, he failed in three marriages. See Paul Johnson, *Intellectuals* (1988), chapter 8. —JSB

32. We are not far from it. The United States Supreme Court, and myriad lower courts, have concluded that the law "evolves." What that means is, the law is not fixed, but is whatever a particular judge at a particular time wants it to be.—JSB

33. Busby is referring to the empirically proven phenomenon known as "flock fever." This is the strong tendency to side with "conventional wisdom" no matter what the factual underpinnings of that wisdom. Facts don't matter; one's appearance before one's peers is the main concern.—JSB

34. At this time in America's history, the First Amendment's guarantee of free speech had not been tested and refined in the courts, and was little discussed. Today it is one of our cherished privileges. Unless, of course, one happens to be a political conservative at Harvard, Yale, or Dartmouth.—JSB

35. "Fundamentalism" draws its name from a series of booklets published between 1910 and 1915. Titled "The Fundamentals," these volumes were scholarly defenses of the Christian faith against various forms of error. In well-written terms, "The Fundamentals" upheld the inerrancy of

Scripture, the virgin birth, Christ's substitutionary atonement, the bodily resurrection of Christ, and the historicity of miracles. The caricature of "Fundamentalists" as rabid, anti-intellectual zealots is belied by these texts. What is interesting to note historically is that today we have a species known as "Darwinian Fundamentalists," who are often anti-intellectual and extreme for their own cause. —JSB

36. A reference to German Higher Criticism, a self-defeating intellectual movement of the nineteenth century. Amazingly, some today still approach the Bible with these antiquated presuppositions. —JSB

37. This truth would prove itself over time, most notably in the 1973 decision *Roe v. Wade,* in which the Supreme Court decided to take an invented right called "privacy" (not enumerated in the Constitution) and extend it into a right to destroy pre-born life. The proof of Sir Max's judgment that "digestion" and "wanting" to decide are paramount in current "evolutionary law" comes from the author of *Roe,* Justice Harry Blackmun. It is now well known he was primarily influenced not by the text of the Constitution (as a Justice of the Court is supposed to be), but by his wife and daughters nagging him into submission (see Woodward and Armstrong, *The Brethren).* —JSB

38. The ACLU's goal was to get the law declared unconstitutional so evolution could be offered as an alternative theory in the classroom. Ironically, in the 1980s, the ACLU would fight to have evolution taught as the *only* theory, censoring creationism from the schools. Afraid that children might make up their own minds, the ACLU

sought to limit the flow of information. This tactic became one of their most important. For instance, in fighting informed consent laws they determined that women should not have access to all the information about abortion, lest they actually learn something that might lead them to halt the procedure. —JSB

39. Busby, of course, could not have foreseen the takeover of journalism by political liberals, the most gullible of modern people. Many of these would end up writing editorials for the *New York Times*. —JSB

40. This historical datum was apparently lost on the authors of the play, *Inherit the Wind,* a well-written though propagandistic outburst of anti-religious flatulency. Do not get your truth from the American theater. —JSB

41. Scopes was fined $100. The judgment was reversed on appeal. —JSB

42. This view is corroborated by Marcet Haldeman-Julius, who was present with the Darrow defense team at their quarters immediately after the Bryan cross-examination. In a 1927 recollection, Haldeman-Julius reported that Darrow "sat tranquilly on the porch of the Mansion. He looked, to use a familiar but ever expressive simile, like the full and contented cat that had just eaten the canary." —JSB

43. Renamed Planned Parenthood Federation of America in 1953. —JSB

44. *Flapper*—a lively, active young woman, cynical about society and sexually free (U.S. colloquial). From Richard A. Spears, *Slang and Euphemism*. There are no more flappers. Today, there are "Wellesley students." —JSB

45. This was prophetic. As courts of law in America floated further and further away from the very idea of "law," which presupposes a Supreme Law Giver, and drifted toward other ways of imposing rule on society, many judges and legislators would subscribe to an economic theory of law, under which a cost/benefit analysis is undertaken in every dispute. Thus, moral fault is no longer relevant. We only look to "deep pockets" and the distribution of money. —JSB

46. Though rare, this dealing in spirits is not without precedent. See 1 Samuel 28:7-20 for a biblical example.—JSB